Green SMOOTHIE Joy

Recipes for Living, Loving, and Juicing Green

Cressida Elias

Skyhorse Publishing

Skyhorse Publishing books may be purchased in bulk at special discounts for sales promotion, corporate gifts, fund-raising, or educational purposes. Special editions can also be created to specifications. For details, contact the Special Sales Department, Skyhorse Publishing, 307 West 36th Street, 11th Floor, New York, NY 10018 or info@skyhorsepublishing.com.

Skyhorse® and Skyhorse Publishing® are registered trademarks of Skyhorse Publishing, Inc. ®, a Delaware corporation.

www.skyhorsepublishing.com

Cataloging-in-Publication Data available on file.

10 9 8 7 6 5 4 3 2

ISBN: 978-1-62087-293-2

Printed in the United States of America

Medical Disclaimer: The information in this book is intended solely as general information for the reader. It is not to be used to diagnose health problems or for treatment purposes. It is not a substitute for medical care provided by a licensed and qualified health professional.

Contents

Introduction

We are more aware than ever of the reasons why we should eat healthy. And we know that whatever we put into our bodies we are going to get out of them in terms of energy and health benefits.

But with our busy lifestyles, it is often very hard to eat good food on the go and most of us tend to pick up fast food, unhealthy snacks, or packaged food to save time. Getting that "five a day" serving of fruit and veggies can prove to be a difficult task!

That is where smoothies and juices, prepared fresh in your kitchen, can help solve the problem.

I am always amazed and excited at the variations of fruit and veggies you can put into a blender or juicer to create a delicious smoothie that is easy to drink. For example, just adding two large handfuls of spinach into a juicer or blender will add some bright green and a lot of nutrition to your smoothie! But if you took the same amount and added it to a salad instead—well, you would probably find it hard to munch through it all in one sitting!

Some people add extra ingredients such as protein powders or oats to make a satisfying meal out of a smoothie, saving cooking time! Some people just use greens and fruit for a mealtime smoothie and find it perfectly nourishing.

So smoothies are now the new "fast food" and you can even buy blenders with jugs that double as cups so you just blend and go…so what are you waiting for?

You many think that drinking several cups of store-bought fruit juice from the supermarket or café should supply your body with enough vitamins. However, most of these juices have added sugar or sweeteners, or are from concentrate, or have colors and "natural flavors" added, and have all been pasteurized.

To explain briefly:

Sugar can come in a variety of forms such as cane sugar, white sugar, beet sugar, corn syrup, dextrose, fructose, succanat, sucrose, and so on. Taken in excess, these forms of sugar can lead to problems with increased insulin (a hormone) levels in your body which in turn affects your blood sugar levels. Too much insulin creates insulin resistance, which is associated with obesity, fatigue, high blood pressure, diabetes, and other diseases. Also, excessive ingestion of these sugars will exhaust your pancreas and adrenal function. Still want your sugary fruit juice?

Artificial sweeteners are not recommended—natural sweeteners such as stevia and xylitol, if you must have them, are recommended instead.

Obviously, many colors and "natural flavors" in store-bought juice are artificial—some people are particularly sensitive to them—and they are not something you want (or need) to be taking when you are going for extra nutrition!

Pasteurization – normal or flash (meaning very fast) kills bacteria and prolongs the life of the juice (important for supermarkets) but this process can also cause a loss of nutrients and important enzymes.

Concentrated – this is when a fruit is squeezed, the water taken out of it so it can be transported more easily, then the water added back later. Micronutrients such as antioxidants are thought to be lost in this process.

So to *really* get the most out of your fruits and veggies, and unless you can go to a juice bar and watch them make your juice, you need to make your own and drink it as soon as possible while completely fresh. When a smoothie calls for juice, make your own and then add to the blender. This does of course mean you need to buy a juicer or get a combined blender and juicer—we'll get to that later.

The question has been raised as to whether green smoothie enthusiasts drink too *many* greens and that this could become toxic to the body. There is no evidence that anyone has become sick from drinking nutrient-filled smoothies, however; everything in moderation. If you consumed only green smoothies every day then your diet would not be balanced and you would be creating other health problems for yourself—but this is just common sense.

A few green smoothie benefits

They can help detox and cleanse your body to generally improve your health or help heal conditions such as acne.

Smoothies give real energy kicks and make a nice caffeine replacement.

They are fast and easy to make and you can blend and go. You can also make and store them in the fridge for about two to three days.

You can pack a smoothie with different fruits and veggies you probably would not eat all in one day.

Kids enjoy making them and drinking them, so you can hide some veggies under the taste of their favorite fruits.

They are packed with enzymes and vitamins. The essential nutrient in greens (chlorophyll) helps to purify your blood and helps to eliminate bad breath and body odor and is great for anemia.

The antioxidants and phytochemicals present in veggies give you energy for a healthy snack or a meal replacement if you are dieting.

Greens are alkaline; this is great for your health as ingesting alkaline food will help balance your acid/alkaline level, which can help prevent or heal many different health problems.

I hope you enjoy this book as much as I have enjoyed writing it. If you are just starting out and making smoothies for the first time, stick to the recipes and when you feel more confident, start to experiment with different fruit and veggie combinations. Good luck!

The Difference between Juicing and Blending

Some people prefer to juice their raw food and others prefer a blended smoothie. They are both nutritious and I will try to explain in brief the benefits of both.

If you put veggies and fruit in a juicer, you will leave the fiber and pulp behind and just get a liquid full of vitamins, enzymes, and lots of micronutrients, including the raw food "x factor" that will definitely give you a buzz. Some people prefer the liquid because the body is able to absorb the nutrients in minutes rather than a couple of hours because there is no fiber or pulp to slow down digestion.

If you throw fruit and greens into a blender then you will be getting a more fulfilling drink because the "meat" of the food is still in the drink, but the cell walls have been broken down to a more digestible (liquid) form that you couldn't accomplish on your own unless you chewed for hours! So you will still benefit from all the nutrients that the fruit or vegetable has to offer. However, drink your smoothie slowly as your body still needs time to digest the fiber and drinking them too quickly can cause bloating. Rest assured that once you start sipping a green smoothie, your body will begin absorbing the nutrients immediately. Fiber is important for your body as it helps the elimination of waste, which is vital for cleaning out your colon. Drinking two or three green smoothies a day will fill you up and supply your body with essential vitamins and minerals.

Just having one juice and one smoothie a day can get you incredible results—increased health, vitality, and weight loss.

Bear in mind that if you come across a smoothie recipe that requires juice—make the juice yourself. That way you can be assured of its freshness.

Fruits are considered "cleansing" and veggies are "nourishing," so ideally you'll want to get both fruit and veggies into your smoothies. But sometimes you may just crave a fruity snack or treat—nothing wrong with that!

Generally, green smoothies are approximately 60 percent fruit and 40 percent vegetables, which makes them taste a lot better than 100 percent vegetable juices because the fruit content makes them a bit sweeter.

However, once you get used to the "green" taste, you can reduce the fruit and increase the vegetables in the smoothie to rebuild and regenerate your body faster. Try and aim for a 50:50 split or even less fruit, particularly if you are sensitive to sugar or have yeast and candida problems. Fruit sugar will raise your blood sugar levels, so if you are drinking lots of smoothies, you are going to want to use low-sugar fruit such as berries rather than very sweet fruit such as grapes and bananas.

For a sweeter taste without using fruit, try a carrot—juice it or add it whole to the blender. You will be surprised at how sweet it is!

Some people experience an unpleasant "detox" feeling when starting to juice or blend for the first time. This feeling will pass after a short while, and certainly blending greens rather than simply juicing them will minimize this effect as the absorption rate is a little slower. That is why some people prefer green smoothies over green juices.

Most green smoothie enthusiasts recommend you rotate your green veggies to ensure a balanced vegetable intake.

One more reason some people favor smoothies—the blender is easier to clean! Juicers usually have several parts, but a blender just has a jug that can be washed quickly. If you are rushing out the door you can definitely throw your ingredients into a blender, whizz it, pour, and run out of the house with minimal mess left behind.

However, if you are juicing you will have to clean the juicer, but if you rinse the parts straight away, the clean-up isn't too time-consuming. My juicer has only five parts that come apart easily and can be replaced without much hassle.

Blenders, Smoothie Makers, and Juicers

Blenders and smoothie makers are one and the same, although some products are simply called blenders, whereas others are named smoothie makers—often the smoothie maker will have a tap on it to enable easier pouring.

Blenders can be used for a wide variety of recipes including delicious soups so if you are going to invest in a new machine, I'd get a versatile one. I recommend getting the most powerful blender that your budget will allow—look for one with at least 600w but preferably 1000w. If the blender has advanced cutting action and high revolutions per minute (RPM) then you are good to go. You need a strong blender so that the greens in your smoothies are completely broken down—makes for easier drinking and it ensures all the nutrients are released.

Low-wattage motors may burn out quickly, so go for the highest quality you can. Remember—even with 1000w blenders you need to begin your blending at a LOW SPEED before moving to high speed to prevent smoking and burn-out. When you see your smoothie is thoroughly mixed but with a few bits left you can take the speed up to blend it completely.

Many blenders have a pulsing action or an ice-crushing button, which is also very useful for those icy cool smoothies in the summer! Even adding a couple of ice cubes to your smoothie ensures that the mixture will remain cool—some people find that blending heats up the ingredients, so ice cubes are essential.

Vitamix or Blendtec brand machines are great for smoothies; however, these blenders are not cheap and many people are finding blenders for less that are just as good. I use a Villaware BLVLLAZ05H 2 Litre Jug Blender with a 1000w motor. This blender cost me around $150 and my green smoothies are perfectly blended. It also looks great in the kitchen and is extremely sturdy and easy to clean.

Juicers can be bought separately or can come with a blender. These days, juicers are pretty easy to clean with only a few parts to assemble. I use a Philips brand centrifugal juicer, and although it is a little more bulky than a blender, it does a good job.

I recommend a centrifugal juicer—these are high-speed, cheap, and juice very quickly. Some people prefer a masticating juicer or twin-gear one, which basically juices at low speeds by crushing, and gets more juice out of a vegetable than a centrifugal one. These juicers also don't aerate the juice like the centrifugal ones, meaning you can keep the juice in the fridge longer before it spoils. The high-speed juicers will make juice that you should drink straight away. Also, some people say the high speed juicers heat the juice and reduce the enzyme activity of it. I personally haven't found this to be a problem but I suggest you look into it if you are concerned.

The Origin of Smoothies and the Green Smoothie

Smoothies have actually been around since the 1930s when the first Waring blender was invented. Smoothies then were just blended fruit and ice, but adding yogurt or milk became more popular in the '60s and '70s. Thereafter, with the help of the growing fitness industry, smoothies became even more popular and all sorts of new ingredients were added to the mix—including protein powder, wheatgrass, etc.

In the last few years green smoothies have been gaining a lot of popularity due to their incredible health benefits (and great taste!). They were popularized by raw food diet practitioner Victoria Boutenko. She was interested in how eating large amounts of green leafy vegetables could have an effect on her family's health.

She learned that chimpanzees who have an almost identical DNA structure to humans, were more resistant to common diseases such as cancer, AIDS, and heart disease. She discovered that while the standard US diet was comprised of only 3 percent green veggies, in the diet of a chimpanzee green veggies amounted to a whopping 39 percent. Thus, Victoria started to make smoothies with lots of veggies to increase the greens in her diet (blending the greens down meant you could drink a lot more than you would be able to eat). And so the Green Smoothie was born.

Dr. Ann Wigmore, who was an early pioneer of a raw and natural food diet, made a comparison between a molecule of chlorophyll (from green leafy veggies) to a molecule of human blood—the idea being that ingesting chlorophyll is like receiving a healthy blood transfusion!

Of course, the green smoothie became very popular, not least because it was easy to drink your daily dose of green veggies, but also because kids love them, and people see huge health benefits from drinking them—from increased health and energy to weight loss.

There are so many combinations you can make with fruit and veggies that you won't ever get bored. It doesn't matter if you stick to the same few fruit and veggies if you are reliant on what your local farm shop and superstore have in stock. You can still add other ingredients like oats or flax seed, etc. for different tastes and nutritional needs.

Using Frozen Fruit

You can freeze fresh fruit or buy frozen packaged fruit (I love using frozen berries, for example) and use these in a smoothie—the frozen fruit creates a cool, thicker smoothie and you probably won't need to add extra ice. Bananas are particularly good frozen—peel them when they are ripe and full of vitamins and minerals, not when they are hard and just starchy—slice them, freeze on a bit of foil then store in the freezer in a freezer bag or container. Now you can add a few slices of banana each morning instead of having to use a whole one each time, if you wish to change the amount of fruit in your smoothies.

For other large fruits like melons, chop them up as well and freeze on a plate or some foil first before putting them all together in a bag and leaving in the freezer.

Basic Ingredients and Essential Tips for Making Green Smoothies

Healthy smoothies need a base for creaminess, some liquid, then the fruit and/or veggies, plus added ingredients for extra nutrition.

For the base, most green and other smoothie makers use either banana, avocado, and/or mango or papaya to make them creamy. For other fruit smoothies you can use yogurt for a creamy texture and for extra bulk and nutrition you can add oats to any smoothie. Alternately, nuts make a great base as they are extremely creamy when you blend them with some water.

Bananas are great when they are ripe. That is when they have a few black and brown spots on them and are full of vitamins and minerals. They contain fiber, vitamin A, C, E, K, thiamine, riboflavin, niacin, B6, folate, B12, and pantothenic acid. A banana will really add a sweeter taste to your smoothie and cover up a lot of the green taste. It may also solidify after an hour or so and you could serve up a green smoothie dessert!

To make green smoothies palatable for kids, add more banana, mango, or frozen berries—the sweetness will keep the greens hidden.

For other fruit smoothies you can use yogurt, cream, or creme fraiche for a creamy texture. Some people prefer not to use dairy for health reasons and I personally have chosen to go dairy free for weight loss and as a healthier choice but please do your own research on this subject. For extra bulk and nutrition you can also add oats to any smoothie.

If you want to avoid fruit, then avocados give a thick texture to a smoothie and provide vital nutrients and phytochemicals—just make sure they are ripe (not black and dented).

A note on avocados and fat content

I use avocados in most of the recipes because they are great for adding thickness to a smoothie and are nutrient-dense. They contain all 18 essential amino acids and thus are a complete protein that is easy to digest. They also contain "healthy fat" which boosts the so-called "good" cholesterol, which helps protect against free radical damage and diabetes. They are rich in carotenoids (for eye health) and are anti-inflammatory. The main fat in avocados is oleic acid, which actually is shown to improve heart health. They also contain many omega-3 fatty acids, which are known to lower risk of heart disease. The fat content that you may be worried about is the *good* kind of fat!

If you are starting a healthy diet, trying to lose weight, or going "raw," one or two avocados a day can actually help you make the transition as they will fill you up and curb your cravings. My advice is to simply listen to your body. As you get healthier you may need less or prefer less good fat in your diet or you may not. Limit your bad fat intake or give it up altogether. You can easily adjust the amount of avocado you use in a green smoothie according to your needs—less if you are just having a snack smoothie, more if you are using it as a meal replacement. I love the taste of avocado in my smoothies but if you don't, then decrease the amount to a quarter of an avocado and add more banana or mango.

Using mango and/or pineapple and coconut milk together will give you a tropical taste to any smoothie.

For a boost to the nutritional value of a smoothie, you can add wheatgrass powder, whey, or other protein powders, maca, flax seeds, or other green powders like spirulina. Just adding one of these will add more "energy" to the smoothie, so have a couple handy (see chapter on superfoods).

You can try other liquids in your smoothie other than cow's milk and water. Almond milk, hemp milk, juiced veggies or fruit, and coconut milk as suggested above, will all add a different taste and consistency.

Green smoothie enthusiasts will go out looking for green leaves in gardens themselves and pick edible leaves and blend them up. You really do have to know what is edible and what is not to do this. I would advise you not to do this unless you are 110 percent sure of what you are picking, as some leaves are poisonous. I would stick to what you can get locally from markets and shops and keep an eye out for in-season produce to change up your routine. There will not be any recipes in this book with hard-to-find ingredients!

Other ingredients to have handy are honey, maple syrup, the sugar substitute xylitol, or the sweet herb stevia. However you should only need these if you are not using much fruit but you wish to have a little sweetness to your smoothie. The juice of carrot, beetroot, pomegranate or extra berries or banana should give you enough sweetness without resorting to sweeteners.

Herbs and Seeds

Herbal teas are a great addition to smoothies. You could try brewing some ginger tea, chamomile tea, nettle tea, or green tea and adding the liquid to reach the desired consistency. Alternately, you can find fresh herbs from your local store and add them directly to your smoothie!

Basil goes well with mango or with apples, carrots, and berries.

Chia seed is a member of the mint family and is an very old food used in the diet of the Mayan, Aztec, and Southwest Native American people. Chia is the highest plant source of omega-3, which is an essential fat we don't get enough of in the Western diet, so by adding just a tablespoon to your smoothies you will be doing yourself a world of good. It also helps thicken a thin smoothie instead of using extra banana or avocado, etc. If you get the seed already milled then you won't need to worry about an extra crunch in your smoothie.

Cilantro (also called coriander) is good with pineapple, strawberries, and bananas and is known for its great health benefits—including removing toxic metals from the body, cleansing the liver, acting as a natural antiseptic, and providing a good source of iron, vitamin C, and magnesium.

Flax seed (or linseed) is high in fiber, phytochemicals, and omega-3. It is best if this is already milled. There is a small amount of cyanide in flax seed; however, it appears in such low amounts that it's not a health concern—usually flax seed consumption is about 1 or 2 tablespoons a day.

Hemp seeds are another source of omega-3, vitamins, protein, and minerals. Again, find it milled as it's easier to blend.

Mint is great with melon, kiwi, or strawberries and gives the smoothie a little extra freshness to it. Mint contains vitamins A, C, and B2 and various essential minerals such as manganese, copper, iron, etc.

Parsley is great in green smoothies—it really packs a good vitamin punch with iron, protein, calcium, beta-carotene, and other trace vitamins and minerals such as magnesium, potassium, and zinc. It's very low in calories but is high in fiber. As the herb is quite pungent it is best to use it sparingly and combine it with other greens such as kale and spinach. Fruits that go with parsley are pear with kiwi or pineapple and mango with oranges.

Pumpkin seeds are packed with fiber, vitamins, and minerals and also the free radical-fighting antioxidants. They also contain protein so they're great in a mealtime smoothie.

Sprouted seeds are a great source of nutrition—and you can even sprout your own if you feel ambitious. Alfalfa, broccoli, lentil, mung bean, wheatgrass, and pea-sprouted seeds are just some examples.

Sprouted seeds contain many nutrients such as vitamins, protein, minerals, and enzymes. They have fiber and are alkalizing for your body, which is great for your health. They contain both iron and vitamin C and give your immune system a good kick.

Sunflower seeds are quite nutty and high in calories full of good nutrients such as vitamins, particularly vitamin E, minerals, and of course antioxidants. They also are a good protein source. Various benefits of eating these seeds are: a reduced blood sugar level, decrease in anxiety, and lower LDL cholesterol levels.'

It's a good idea to soak nuts and seeds for a few hours or overnight before using them in smoothies. They will blend better, plus more of their nutrition is released with soaking.

Suggested Superfoods

A superfood is a term to describe foods that are densely packed with nutrients and should be included in your diet. I often use a ready-made powder comprised of something like green barley grass or wheatgrass. However, if you are juicing and blending lots of fruit and veggies every day you should not really need extra superfood powder. That said, some people might need an extra boost. It's also handy if you are out of green veggies or just want to make something fruity but add a little "green."

There is a huge list of foods now that are generally referred to as "super," but here are some that you can easily find and include in a smoothie:

Blueberries

High in fiber and antioxidants, blueberries are a top superfood.

Blue-green algae

Comes in powder form and is the richest source of chlorophyll known to man. It is a substance that basically cleans your blood and detoxifies. Also a great source of protein, beta-carotene, and B12.

Brazil nuts

A great way to get a good dose of selenium, zinc, protein, magnesium, and thiamine. You can throw a couple of these into the blender every now and then and they will smooth out well. I have seen it recommended that you don't eat more than 1 or 2 brazil nuts a day because of their high selenium content; they can become toxic in high doses, and also raise your LDL cholesterol.

Cacao

Raw chocolate, an extremely rich antioxidant and packed with iron, magnesium, and chromium as well. It is said to raise your mood, lower cholesterol, and improve the circulation of your blood. Cacao also contains phenethylamine which is reported to create greater focus and make you more alert. The phytochemicals in cacao are said to be an aphrodisiac. Bear in mind it does contain some caffeine as well. You can usually get cacao nibs or powder in your local health store. Will make your smoothie chocolatey!

Coconut

Good for energy, burning fat, and is a good source of fiber, iron, and manganese. It is also reported to improve your thyroid function.

Guava

This is packed full of vitamin C, plus fiber, potassium, manganese, and folic acid.

Maca

Often referred to as Incan superfood, it has been used for thousands of years by Andean societies to nourish and heal. Benefits include increased stamina, endurance, and libido, and it is also said to stimulate tired adrenals and the entire endocrine system to restore vitality. It contains amino acids, minerals, vitamins, alkaloids, and sterols (great for body builders!). It has a vanilla/caramel taste and is great in smoothies.

Mesquite Powder

Some people put this in their smoothies. It is ground from the pods in the mesquite plant and has been eaten for thousands of years by Native Americans. It is rich in protein, fiber, potassium, iron, zinc, calcium, and lysine, and is apparently very good at balancing blood sugar because the sugar within it is a fructose and does not require insulin to metabolise it.

As a side note, if you are diabetic or hypoglycemic, green smoothies can help your condition. You can stick to just veggies, tomato, and avocado, no fruit or very low sugar fruit, and add milled flax seed, flax seed oil, or hemp seed oil to your smoothies, which helps slow down the digestion and release of sugars.

Pomegranate

Full of antioxidants as well and the seeds contain fiber. Its benefits include: prevention of blood clots, reported to be a natural cure for prostate cancer, can prevent heart problems, reduces diarrhea, reduces plaque in arteries, lowers blood pressure, and many more.

Raspberries

High in fiber, antioxidants, and other nutrients.

Spirulina

This is a type of blue-green algae and a wonderful source of protein, essential fatty acids, minerals, and vitamins. The iron is beneficial for those with anemia. It is said to help with weight loss, detoxify your body, improve blood sugar problems, remove toxic metals from the body, and lower cholesterol, among other benefits.

Wheatgrass

This is good for chlorophyll, enzymes, amino acids, minerals, and vitamins. Benefits include increasing red blood cell count, lowering blood pressure, helping to detoxify the body, neutralizing toxins, and alkalizing the body. It will strengthen your cells, is said to restore fertility, turn gray hair to normal color, and even freshen your breath!

This is just a short list of the many superfoods available to you. If you check out your local health food store you will be sure to find various superfoods in powder form that will provide your smoothie with that extra nutrient boost.

About Milks: Buy or Make Your Own?

Adding milk is a great option for your smoothies. It will help create a creamier and thicker consistency than just adding water. So go ahead and happily add some organic cow's milk, goat milk, hemp seed milk, or almond milk to your next creation.

Cow's milk has come under scrutiny recently with some health professionals now saying it's bad for us and only baby cows should drink it! However, some health practitioners say that organic raw milk is fine to drink because it is unpasteurised and the healthy bacteria and enzymes are still intact and no artificial growth hormones are present. I have seen reports of dairy being linked to cancer as well, so I wouldn't want to recommend it but if you do use it, don't go overboard. Goat's milk is said to be much healthier. Do your own research but I personally gave up dairy to lose extra weight and be healthier and didn't find it hard at all as I use coconut milk, almond milk, and water instead. This book does have yogurt smoothie recipes because I figured everyone wants a treat sometimes and if probiotic yogurts are used, you will get a good dose of healthy bacteria!

When you buy almonds, make sure they are the sweet variety that have been pasteurized, as opposed to raw almonds—these are a safer choice.

You can use brazil nut milk in moderation—as aforementioned, brazil nuts can be toxic is large doses. I suggest making a small amount of brazil nut milk and using sparingly; alternatively, pop a brazil nut or two in your smoothie once a day or every now and then.

Hemp seeds are great for protein as they contain eight amino acids and therefore are a "complete" protein. They contain a high amount of omega-3 fatty acids, vitamins, and minerals. Hemp milk I find, though, is an acquired taste!

Pumpkin seeds also make a good milk.

You can find oat, nut, and seed milks in the store, but if you want to make your own, then use this procedure:

Soak your nuts overnight before blending. (Hemp seeds don't need soaking; just rinse). Rinse the soaked seeds or nuts.

Take a cup of your choice of seeds or nuts.

Put in a blender and add three to four cups of filtered or pure water.

Add one or two dates or a little honey, xylitol, stevia, agave nectar, or cinnamon plus a little vanilla extract—these are all optional depending on your taste.

Blend and then pour through a sieve or strainer and for even better straining, put through a cheesecloth.

This will give you a thick milk.

For a thinner consistency, add more water in the original mix or blend with the strained milk.

Refrigerate and store as normal milk but shake before use in case of separation.

List of Fat-Burning Foods and Using Smoothies for Weight Loss

Without a doubt you can lose weight drinking green smoothies! Replace your daily snacks of cookies, potato chips, or other unhealthy foods with a smoothie for a great start to healthy eating and weight loss.

I lost approximately seven pounds in two weeks just from replacing breakfast or lunch with a green smoothie. I usually made enough for two or three glasses so what I didn't consume at that meal-time I had later as a snack. The great thing about smoothies is that once you start drinking them you will notice that you won't feel so hungry for unhealthy snacks, your energy will last longer, and it will become even easier to cut back on breakfast or lunch. You will probably be ready for a good evening meal though—make sure it's healthy!

To accelerate your fat burning, try fat-burning foods in your smoothies— check out the following list:

Apples

They are full of soluble fiber called pectin which help you feel fuller for longer.

Apples also contain Vitamin C.

Apricots

Rich in fiber, apricots help you feel fuller longer and will help to lower blood cholesterol levels. They contain a lot of beta-carotene, which helps mop up free radicals and improve your immune system.

Beets

Beets are a natural diuretic—this means they will help flush out excess water weight or fluid. They have iron, fiber, and natural chlorine, which will help rinse toxins and fats out of your body. Because of the iron content in beets they are a great food for people with anemia.

Broccoli

Broccoli is full of fiber as well, and rich in vitamin C, which will dilute the fat and makes it easier to flush from your body. Contains vitamin B, calcium, iron, beta-carotene, and can help lower blood pressure and detox your liver. Use only a few florets per smoothie because it is quite bitter tasting—you can juice it first and add it for extra "green."

Blackberries

Full of fiber, vitamin C, and other nutrients.

Blueberries

Blueberries are considered a great stomach fat fighter. They are full of phytonutrients, antioxidants, and are low-calorie if you are being careful. They are a low-sugar fruit, so they are a good option if you are sensitive to sugar.

Cabbage

Sulfur and iodine in cabbage help cleanse your stomach and intestines. Cabbage also contains calcium and vitamin C.

Cantaloupe

Good for vitamin A and C, potassium, vitamin B6, dietary fiber, folate, and niacin (vitamin B3), and fiber.

Carrots

Makes a very sweet juice to add to smoothies, they are high in vitamin A and are a good detoxifier, and help your liver and guts function smoothly.

Celery

This will eliminate carbon dioxide from your system and its pure form of calcium will feed your endocrine system. Hormones from this part of your body help to break up fats. Contains magnesium and iron and is a natural diuretic.

Cherries

Obviously remove the stone before blending! They are supposed to reduce pain and inflammation and contain anthocyanin which is said to contribute to belly fat reduction.

Chives

Help with weight loss due to their high chromium content. Chromium is a nutrient that improves the good functioning of insulin in the bloodstream. Basically the more stable your insulin, the more stable your blood sugar levels and the more stable your energy is, leading to less cravings!

Cranberries

Low in sugar, plus great for the urinary and digestive tract. Great for fighting cellulite and detoxifying your body.

Cucumbers

A great fat-burner because as a diuretic, they will encourage the removal of waste fluids from your body. They also have good amounts of silica and sulfur to stimulate the kidneys to flush out uric acid in the body. Good for nails, skin, and hair, and can reduce blood pressure.

Dandelion greens

Dandelion leaves and roots are used to treat various ailments and boost health by Europeans, Asians, and Native Americans. The greens stimulate the liver, kidneys, and digestion, and act as a diuretic.

Goji berries

Fantastic for antioxidants and contain protein, essential minerals, and amino acids. You can buy these dried. Great for blood building and the immune system.

Grapefruit

Grapefruit will help the body's insulin levels to contribute to a fat-loss regime.

Green beans

Low in calories, rich in minerals. Improve liver, kidney, and lung functions. Green beans have vitamin C and iron, which both fight fat.

Honeydew melon

Great for fiber and for high water content, so will boost your hydration on a hot day, plus deliver vitamins and minerals to your body.

Juniper berries

Help eliminate excess water retention and improve digestion. They are also anti-inflammatory! **Not to be consumed by pregnant women or women wishing to conceive as juniper can cause uterine contractions.**

Kale

Kale is a member of the same family as brussel sprouts and broccoli. Very high in fiber and contains many nutrients, so great for dieters.

Lettuce

Full of vitamins and minerals and good for your metabolism with

thermogenic properties. (Thermogenic fruits and veggies are low in calories but require a lot of energy to digest, thus raising your metabolism after you eat them, which helps you burn more fat.)

Lemons

A squeeze of lemon is great for breaking down fat and cleansing the body.

Limes

Packed with fat-fighting vitamin C!

Mango

Packed with fiber but low in calories, a good source of beta-carotene and vitamin C.

Nectarine

Has protein, fiber, and is full of nutrients. The calcium, magnesium, and potassium promote fluid balance, so they are good for weight loss.

Oatmeal

Adding some oatmeal to a smoothie can help you lose weight as it is high in fiber, which will help stabilize your blood sugar, so you are less likely to snack on unhealthy snacks.

Orange

Great for their high vitamin C content and fiber.

Papaya

Papaya is fat-free and contains fiber, A, C, potassium, calcium, iron, thiamine, riboflavin, and niacin. Also contains the enzyme peptin, which helps dissolve fat in the body. Please buy organic as papaya is often genetically modified.

Peaches

Packed with vitamins and nutrients and fiber. They are full of fiber, which makes them filling.

Pears

Contain a very high fiber content with vitamin C and calcium.

Pineapple

Pineapples contain the enzyme bromelain, which helps digest protein and is also anti-inflammatory. They are also a good source of fiber, thiamine, vitamin B6, copper, vitamin c, and manganese.

Pumpkin seeds

Also called pepitas, these are delicious crunchy snacks that are rich in manganese, tryptophan, magnesium,

and phosphorus. They are thought to be anti-inflammatory agents as well.

Raspberries

The raspberry is good fat buster because of its high fiber content and low sugar level. The pectin in raspberries will help prevent too much fat from being absorbed into your cells, thus helping weight loss.

Spinach

Packed with iron, it will boost your metabolism when eaten regularly and will promote better liver function.

Strawberries

Packed with powerful antioxidants, plus they also help reduce inflammation and increase metabolism. Can help control blood sugar levels.

Tomato

Good vitamin C content plus contains phytochemicals that produce carnitine. Carnitine helps to break down fat inside your body so it can be used for energy.

Watermelon

Contains loads of fiber and minerals and is great for your metabolism. Watermelons will hydrate you due to their high water content making them great for smoothies.

Other Fruits and Veggies and their Nutritional Value

Avocado

My favorite choice in green smoothies, they are high in protein, potassium, fiber, many vitamins including A, E, C, B6, and K, and healthy unsaturated fats for sustained energy.

Bananas

Contain vitamins, minerals, and antioxidants. Particularly known for their high fiber, high potassium, vitamin C, and B6 content. Great for a quick energy boost due to their simple sugars content.

Coconut

Useful in smoothies as water or milk. Loaded with antioxidant properties, it helps the body with many functions including digestion, cell building, sugar levels, weight loss, and metabolism—and it's antibacterial too. It has a higher concentration of electrolytes than any other food. So great for hydration!

Dates

Contain many vitamins and minerals, particularly high in fiber, iron, potassium, and antioxidant beta-carotene.

Fennel

Good for fiber, vitamins, minerals, and antioxidants.

Ginger

Anti-inflammatory and antibacterial. Helps reduce nausea, migraines, and diarrhea (caused by e. coli). It contains nutrients including vitamins B5 and B6, potassium, magnesium, and manganese.

Grapes

Rich in resveratrol, which is a powerful antioxidant, but they are quite sweet, so be careful if you have a sugar problem.

Passion fruit

Very good source of antioxidants, fiber, vitamins, and minerals, particularly vitamins C, A, and potassium.

Prunes

Very rich in vitamin A and antioxidants. Of course full of fiber and great for constipation!

Kiwi

Great source of vitamin C and E, potassium, and folic acid. Good for blood pressure, heart health, immune system health, and digestion. Will help you feel relief from blockage and bloating.

Red cabbage

Lots of vitamin C and other vitamins and minerals plus fiber.

Sweet bell peppers

Rich source of vitamins and minerals particularly vitamin C in the red pepper, and all contain high vitamin A content. Capsaicin is an alkaloid present in these peppers, which is said to be good for cholesterol levels and is also anti-bacterial, and anti-carcinogenic, with beneficial properties for diabetics.

Other Green Smoothie Greens

Collard greens

A good source of phytonutrients that have anti-cancer properties. Great for vitamins A, K, and C and various minerals.

Mustard greens

Very high in vitamin K, and good for vitamins A and C, plus a high level of folates and fiber.

Rocket or arugula lettuce

Rich in phytochemicals which fight various cancers such as breast, prostate, and ovarian. Contains minerals, particularly calcium and iron plus vitamin K and vitamin C.

Romaine lettuce

Very rich in vitamin A, plus folates, vitamin C and K, B vitamins, and iron.

Swiss chard leaves

A rich source of vitamins A, C, and K plus iron and omega-3 fatty acids. If regularly used, it is said to help iron deficient anemia, prevent osteoporosis and various heart diseases and some cancers.

Turnip greens

Has high levels of antioxidants, vitamins A, C, E, calcium, and copper and is said to be useful for those with arthritis.

Watercress

Great for vitamin A, C, and K, beta-carotene, and various minerals.

You will find many other green veggies in the supermarkets such as spring greens, bok choy, and so on. Feel free to experiment!

Vitamin and Mineral List

I thought it might be beneficial to know the functions of various vitamins and minerals, as I have included approximate nutritional information in certain foods in previous chapters and also in each smoothie recipe. If you are looking to increase your intake of a certain vitamin or mineral, then you can choose a smoothie recipe or certain fruits and veggies accordingly. This list is by no means comprehensive; information can be found in more detail online, but for this book, it should be of some use!

A (retinol)

For vision, skin, bone, tooth growth, etc.

B1 (thiamine)

For good nerve function and metabolism.

B2 (riboflavin)

For metabolism, eyes, and skin. Good for headaches.

B3 (niacin)

For metabolism, skin, nervous system, and digestion.

B6 (pyridoxine)

For metabolism of amino and fatty acid and good for red blood cell production.

Folate

A water-soluble B vitamin that is needed to make DNA and create and maintain cell formation.

B12

Needed to create new cells, break down fatty and amino acids, and good for nerves.

C (ascorbic acid)

Used for collagen creation, amino acid metabolism, great for iron absorption, your immune system, tired adrenals, and it's an antioxidant.

Calcium

Helps to form bones and teeth, and supports blood clotting.

Chloride

Controls the flow of fluids in your blood vessels and tissues and helps regulate body acidity.

Chromium

Helps support insulin and regulate blood sugar levels.

Copper

Helps in the absorption of iron and the formation of hemoglobin.

D

Great for your immune system and for maintaining strong bones and muscles.

E

A great antioxidant, boosts your immune system and widens blood vessels to prevent unwanted blood clotting.

Iodine

Needed by the thyroid, which regulates growth and metabolism.

Iron

Important for energy, and an essential component of hemoglobin that carries oxygen throughout the body.

K

Extremely important in creating proteins that regulate blood clotting, and for bone strengthening.

Magnesium

Used to maintain normal muscle and nerve function, good for the heart and relaxation. It helps keep your immune system healthy, bones strong, and can regulate sugar levels. Good for normal blood pressure and energy metabolism.

Manganese

Supports cell metabolism and protein digestion.

Phosphorus

Essential for bone strength and for the formation of cells.

Potassium

Works with sodium to help maintain water balance in your body, helps control blood pressure, heart rate, and helps with the utilization of energy in the body.

Sodium

Balances your fluids and electrolytes and supports muscles and nerves.

Selenium

Is an antioxidant and helps prevent oxidation in the body.

Zinc

Essential for your immune system, human growth, and enzyme activity.

A note on the vitamin content and nutritional value of each recipe

Below each recipe there is a quick guide to the approximate nutritional value of the smoothie. "High" means that the nutrient is above 20 percent of the daily requirement. Percent Daily Values are based on a diet of 2,000 calories but your diet may include more or less calories depending on your needs. However you can still use the information given to determine whether a smoothie is high in a certain nutrient.

Extra Protein

If you are replacing a meal with a green smoothie, you may wish to add some extra protein in the form of protein powder or a superfood powder. You certainly don't have to, as you may find an avocado in your smoothie provides you with all the energy you need. However some people may feel they need more depending on their age, weight, and activity level.

You might choose to use a whey protein powder—just make sure it is from a good organic source—I use a rice protein powder that is totally satisfying. You may find that some extra nuts and seeds like hemp in your smoothie will be a sufficient amount of protein for you.

You can also throw in some oats for extra energy or protein. Oats are a powerhouse of phytonutrients and these, plus the fiber, help with high blood pressure, sugar level problems, bowel problems, and weight loss, as well as having anti-cancer properties.

Extra Tips for Smoothies

1. Need tips on getting your children to drink nutritious smoothies? This is quite simple—first make it sweet with banana and strawberries, *then* throw in the spinach or lettuce, and finally color it with blueberries, organic chocolate powder, or some raw cacao powder. Remember though—there is caffeine in the cacao and chocolate powder.

2. Add sparkling water for a different effect—both visually and on your taste buds!

3. If your smoothie didn't come out quite as creamy as you had hoped, add an avocado, a banana, or mango. You may also like to add some Greek yogurt with friendly bacteria or nuts to make a creamier texture.

4. Make a green smoothie into a chocolate dessert by adding just greens, plain chocolate powder, avocado, and banana. Refrigerate and it will become like a mousse.

5. Remember to rotate your green veggies for better nutrition. Victoria Boutenko suggests that one should only mix green leaves with fruit, but if using other starchy vegetables such as broccoli, carrots, green beans, cabbage, etc., then it is best to keep fruit out of the smoothie as the combination may cause gas. Or, in my opinion, you can try juicing them and adding them to smoothies for extra vitmins, etc.

6. Add ice while blending to prevent the smoothie from warming up too quickly, or use some frozen fruit.

Ingredient Measurements in the Recipes

This is just a quick note about the measurements in the recipes. One to two cups of liquid will produce about two tall glasses of smoothie. I would start off with one cup of liquid and see how it tastes, then adjust your ingredients accordingly.

All "cups" are an approximate amount and you will need to adjust the measurements according to whether you want your smoothie sweeter, creamier, greener, and so on. There is no right or wrong way to create a smoothie—so have fun!

THE RECIPES

Simply Green and Smooth Recipes

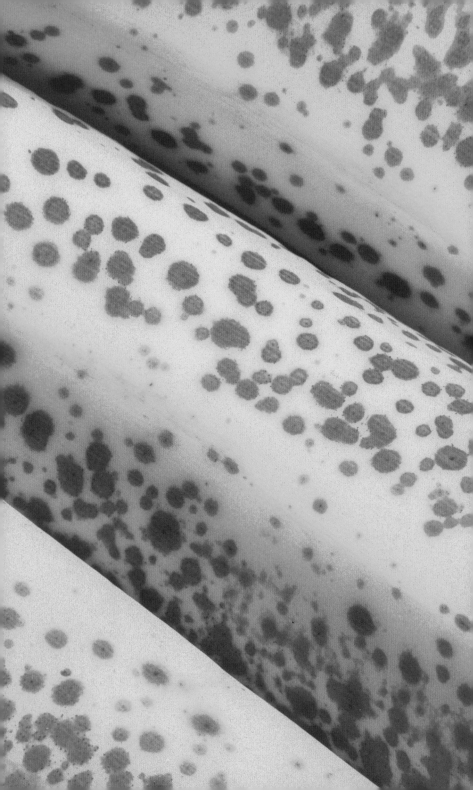

Blue Banana Green Smoothie

1 FROZEN BANANA (RIPE)
A HANDFUL OF BLUEBERRIES
2 INCHES OF CUCUMBER
1–2 CUPS OF ALMOND MILK
A HANDFUL OF BABY SPINACH
1 TSP OR LESS OF HONEY
ICE

OPTIONAL EXTRAS:
A HANDFUL OF WATERCRESS

1. Just throw all ingredients into the blender and starting low, blend well. Add a couple of ice cubes and turn up the blender.

2. Your smoothie will be crunchier if you are using almonds and water instead of almond milk.

NUTRITION:
ENERGY: 397.5 CALORIES
PROTEIN: 12.7 G
CARBS: 84.5 G
FAT: 3.4 G
IRON: 11.8%
HIGH IN B VITAMINS, VITAMIN A, VITAMIN C,
    VITAMIN D, MANGANESE, FOLATE, CALCIUM,
        AND POTASSIUM.

Cacao Green Smoothie

1   FROZEN BANANA
HALF AN APPLE
1   TSP ORGANIC CACAO
    POWDER
2   HANDFULS OF BABY
    SPINACH
1   HEAPED TSP OF FLAX SEED
1–2 CUPS OF WATER

OPTIONAL EXTRAS:
1 TSP CACAO NIBS (WILL BE A
    LITTLE CRUNCHY)
A FEW SCRAPES OF A VANILLA
    POD OR A DASH OF VANILLA
    EXTRACT (SUGAR-FREE)

1. Blend all ingredients. This smoothie might be a
    little thin for your liking so if you want it thicker
    without adding any more ingredients, add some ice
    and blend. Otherwise, add an avocado.

NUTRITION:
ENERGY: 175.8 CALORIES
PROTEIN: 3.2 G
CARBS: 43.7 G
FAT: 1.0 G
IRON: 12.0%
HIGH IN VITAMIN B6, VITAMIN A, VITAMIN C,
        MANGANESE, MAGNESIUM, AND FOLATE.

Berry & Melon Green Smoothie

1 CUP OF RASPBERRIES
A FEW CHUNKS OF
    CANTALOUPE MELON
1 BANANA
2 HANDFULS OF SPRING
    GREENS
1–2 CUPS OF WATER
MAKES 2 GLASSES

OPTIONAL EXTRAS:
A HANDFUL OF SPROUTED
    BROCCOLI OR ALFALFA
    SEEDS

1. Put all the ingredients into the blender and starting low, work your way up to a high speed to really smooth out the spinach leaves.

NUTRITION:
ENERGY: 234.6 CALORIES
PROTEIN: 5.0 G
CARBS: 56.8 G
FAT: 1.5 G
IRON: 14.9%
HIGH IN VITAMIN B6, VITAMIN A , VITAMIN C, AND
    MANGANESE.

Pineapple Detox Green Smoothie

A LITTLE GRATING OF GINGER
1   CUP OF PINEAPPLE
1   AVOCADO
1   INCH OF CUCUMBER
SEVERAL LEAVES OF ROMAINE
    LETTUCE
APPROX 2 CUPS OF WATER

OPTIONAL EXTRAS:
SOME CELERY FOR FURTHER
    DETOXING

1. Start by blending the cucumber and pineapple with
    a little water. Then add the rest of the ingredients
    and speed up the blender to make smooth.

NUTRITION:
ENERGY: 375.5 CALORIES
PROTEIN: 4.9 G
CARBS: 36.2 G
FAT: 27.5 G
IRON: 12.0%
HIGH IN VITAMIN B6, VITAMIN A, VITAMIN C,
    COPPER, FOLATE, MANGANESE, THIAMIN, AND
    PANTOTHENIC ACID.

Green Smoothie Joy!

Zingy Spring Green Smoothie

½ SQUEEZED LEMON
2 HANDFULS OF KALE OR
  SPINACH
1 APPLE
1 FROZEN BANANA
1 AVOCADO
1 TBSP OF CHIA SEEDS
APPROX 1–2 CUPS OF WATER
1 CUP OF ICE

1. Blend all ingredients apart from ice until smooth—
   then add the ice and smooth it up.

NUTRITION:
ENERGY: 484.8 CALORIES
PROTEIN: 4.9 G
CARBS: 65.8 G
FAT: 27.5 G
IRON: 9.4%
HIGH IN VITAMIN B6, VITAMIN C, CALCIUM, FOLATE,
    COPPER, PANTOTHENIC ACID, AND MANGANESE.

Green Smoothie Joy!

Berry Rocket Green Smoothie

1 FROZEN BANANA
1 CUP OF STRAWBERRIES
1 CUP OF BLACKBERRIES
1 HANDFUL OF ROCKET OR
   ARUGULA LETTUCE
ABOUT 2 CUPS OF COCONUT
   MILK
MAKES APPROX 2 GLASSES

1. Put all the ingredients in blender and smooth it.

NUTRITION:
ENERGY: 401.1 CALORIES
PROTEIN: 13.3 G
CARBS: 7.9 G
FAT: 12.0 G
IRON: 96.3%
HIGH IN VITAMIN A, VITAMIN B6, VITAMIN C,
      COPPER, FOLATE, MAGNESIUM, MANGANESE,
      PHOSPHORUS, NIACIN, THIAMIN, AND ZINC.

Pear Delicious Green Smoothie

2   PEARS
1   AVOCADO
1   HANDFUL OF LAMB'S
    LETTUCE
1   HANDFUL OF CORIANDER OR
    CILANTRO
APPROX 2 CUPS OF WATER
1   TSP OF MACA (OPTIONAL)
A LITTLE HONEY IF EXTRA
    SWEETNESS IS NEEDED

1. Blend all ingredients with ice until smooth. Taste
    and if your pears were not the really sweet kind,
    add a little honey.

NUTRITION:
ENERGY: 556.5 CALORIES
PROTEIN: 5.9 G
CARBS: 84.1 G
FAT: 28.2 G
IRON: 16.1%
HIGH IN VITAMIN A, POTASSIUM, VITAMIN B6,
    VITAMIN C, VITAMIN E, COPPER, FOLATE,
    MANGANESE, PANTOTHENIC ACID, NIACIN, AND
    RIBOFLAVIN.

Quick Green Smoothie

1 HANDFUL OF SPINACH
1 SMALL HANDFUL OF
  PARSLEY
1 FROZEN BANANA
1 PAPAYA (SEEDS REMOVED)
A COUPLE ICE CUBES
1–2 CUPS OF WATER

1. Mix all ingredients in a blender until smooth. The parsley tastes quite strong, so add more banana if you are not used to it or make with just a sprig or two.

NUTRITION:
ENERGY: 255.6 CALORIES
PROTEIN: 5.7 G
CARBS: 62.4 G
FAT: 1.6 G
IRON: 96.3%
HIGH IN POTASSIUM, VITAMIN A, VITAMIN B6,
    VITAMIN C, VITAMIN E, FOLATE, MAGNESIUM, AND
        MANGANESE.

Quick Orange Breakfast Green Smoothie

2   LARGE SWISS CHARD
    LEAVES OR LETTUCE LEAVES
1   WHOLE ORANGES WITHOUT
    SEEDS AND PEEL
½   A GRAPEFRUIT WITHOUT
    SEEDS AND PEEL
1   AVOCADO
1   BANANA
OPTIONAL – A SPRINKLE
    OF OATS AND 1 TBSP OF
    VANILLA RICE PROTEIN
    POWDER
ICE CUBES
1 OR 2 CUPS OF WATER

1. Throw in all ingredients and blend—then rush out
    the door!

NUTRITION:
ENERGY: 722.6 CALORIES
PROTEIN: 27.1 G
CARBS: 168.4 G
FAT: 35.0 G
IRON: 153.2%
HIGH IN POTASSIUM, VITAMIN A, VITAMIN B6,
    VITAMIN C, VITAMIN E, CALCIUM, COPPER,
    FOLATE, MAGNESIUM, MANGANESE, NIACIN,
    PANTOTHENIC ACID, RIBOFLAVIN, SELENIUM,
    THIAMIN, AND ZINC.

Orange and Go Green Smoothie

1 ORANGE
1 AVOCADO
1 HANDFUL OF SPINACH
1–2 CUPS OF ALMOND MILK

OPTIONAL EXTRAS:
SOME LETTUCE AND CUCUMBER

1. Blend all together and go!

NUTRITION:
ENERGY: 542.3 CALORIES
PROTEIN: 10.0 G
CARBS: 59.7 G
FAT: 32.0 G
IRON: 15.4%
HIGH IN POTASSIUM, VITAMIN A, VITAMIN B6,
    VITAMIN C, VITAMIN D, CALCIUM, COPPER,
    FOLATE, MAGNESIUM, MANGANESE, NIACIN,
     PANTOTHENIC ACID, RIBOFLAVIN, AND THIAMINE.

Choco Passion Green Smoothie

1   FROZEN BANANA
2   HANDFULS SPINACH
1   PASSION FRUIT (THE
    INSIDES)
2   CHUNKS OF DARK
    CHOCOLATE OR 1 TSP OF
    COCOA POWDER
2   CUPS OF ALMOND MILK
    APPROX

1. Mix all ingredients in a blender.

NUTRITION:
ENERGY: 760.8 CALORIES
PROTEIN: 9.0 G
CARBS: 119.2 G
FAT: 36.1 G
IRON: 29.7%
HIGH IN POTASSIUM, VITAMIN A, VITAMIN B6,
    VITAMIN C, VITAMIN D, CALCIUM, COPPER,
    FOLATE, MAGNESIUM, MANGANESE, AND
        PHOSPHORUS.

Sweet Green Smoothie

2 HANDFULS OF KALE
1 PEAR
1 BANANA
1–2 HANDFULS OF DATES
1 CUP OF WATER
ICE

1. Blend everything together. Add a teaspoon of honey for an even sweeter taste.

NUTRITION:
ENERGY: 374.9 CALORIES
PROTEIN: 7.7 G
CARBS: 92.3 G
FAT: 2.5 G
IRON: 18.8%
HIGH IN POTASSIUM, VITAMIN A, VITAMIN B6,
    VITAMIN C, CALCIUM, COPPER, MAGNESIUM,
        MANGANESE, AND THIAMINE.

Green Smoothie Joy!

Strawberry & Melon Delight Green Smoothie

2   CUPS OF SWISS CHARD
2   CUPS OF WATERMELON
2   INCHES OF CUCUMBER
1   AVOCADO
1   TSP OF CHIA SEED
1   SQUEEZE OF LEMON
1 OR 2 CUPS OF WATER
ICE

1. Mix all ingredients apart from the ice. Blend it well and then add the ice to cool it.

NUTRITION:
ENERGY: 405.4 CALORIES
PROTEIN: 7.4 G
CARBS: 40.3 G
FAT: 28.3 G
IRON: 16.1%
HIGH IN POTASSIUM, VITAMIN A, VITAMIN B6,
    VITAMIN C, COPPER, FOLATE, MAGNESIUM,
    MANGANESE, NIACIN, PANTOTHENIC ACID, AND
        THIAMINE.

Tropical Green Smoothie

1   CUP OF PINEAPPLE CHUNKS
1   CUP OF MANGO
1   HANDFUL OF SPINACH
HALF A CUP OF COCONUT MILK,
    COCONUT WATER, OR SOME
    COCONUT CREAM
SOME WATER
SOME ICE

1. Mix ingredients in a blender until smooth. Add ice at the end. Taste and add more of either coconut or water depending on your preference.

NUTRITION:
ENERGY: 220.1 CALORIES
PROTEIN: 2.8 G
CARBS: 52.3 G
FAT: 2.5 G
IRON: 9.9%
HIGH IN POTASSIUM, VITAMIN A, VITAMIN
    B6, VITAMIN C, VITAMIN E, FOLATE, AND
       MANGANESE.

Green Smoothie Joy!

Wake Up Green Smoothie

1   CUP OF SPINACH
1   STALK CELERY
A CHUNK OF CUCUMBER
1   FROZEN BANANA
1   CUP OF RASPBERRIES
½–1 AVOCADO
1   CUP OF CANTALOUPE
    MELON CHUNKS
1–2 CUPS OF WATER

1. Combine all ingredients and mix until smooth.

NUTRITION:
ENERGY: 537.7 CALORIES
PROTEIN: 8.8 G
CARBS: 40.3 G
FAT: 28.7 G
IRON: 20.4%
HIGH IN POTASSIUM, VITAMIN A, VITAMIN B6,
    VITAMIN C, COPPER, FOLATE, MAGNESIUM,
    MANGANESE, NIACIN, PANTOTHENIC ACID,
        RIBOFLAVIN, AND THIAMINE.

Green Smoothie Joy!

Fruity Power Green Smoothie

2 CUPS OF SWISS CHARD
   OR KALE
A FEW ARUGULA (ROCKET)
   LEAVES
1 KIWI
1 BANANA
1 PEACH (PITTED)
1 TSP OF WHEATGRASS
1–2 CUPS OF WATER

1. Blend all ingredients together until smooth.

NUTRITION:
ENERGY: 216.4 CALORIES
PROTEIN: 5.0 G
CARBS: 53.0 G
FAT: 1.4 G
IRON: 15.9%
HIGH IN POTASSIUM, VITAMIN A, VITAMIN B6,
   VITAMIN C, COPPER, FOLATE, MAGNESIUM, AND
   MANGANESE.

Green Smoothie Joy!

Breakfast Filler Green Smoothie

1   APPLE
½–1 AVOCADO
1   CUP OF BLUEBERRIES
2   HANDFULS OF SPINACH
1   TSP OF CHOCOLATE POWDER
    OR A TBSP OF CACAO NIBS
1   TBSP OF INSTANT OATS (OR
    PRE-BLENDED OATS)
1   CUP OF WATER OR GREEN
    OR WHITE TEA (CHILLED)
SEVERAL ICE CUBES

1. Blend all ingredients together and then add the ice and crush.

NUTRITION:
ENERGY: 525.4 CALORIES
PROTEIN: 8.3 G
CARBS: 79.4 G
FAT: 28.1 G
IRON: 25.9%
HIGH IN POTASSIUM, VITAMIN A, VITAMIN B6,
    VITAMIN C, VITAMIN E, FOLATE, MAGNESIUM,
    MANGANESE, PANTOTHENIC ACID, NIACIN,
    PHOSPHORUS, RIBOFLAVIN, THIAMINE, AND ZINC.

Lunchtime Booster Green Smoothie

1 LARGE SLICE OF PINEAPPLE
3 LEAVES OF ROMAINE
   LETTUCE
½ AVOCADO
1 HANDFUL OF SPINACH
   LEAVES
1 FROZEN BANANA
1 TBSP OF MILLED FLAX SEED
   OR CHIA SEED
1 TSP OF MACA ROOT
2 CUPS OF WATER

1. Blend all ingredients together until smooth. Add more banana for a thicker, sweeter smoothie.

NUTRITION:
ENERGY: 311.7 CALORIES
PROTEIN: 4.8 G
CARBS: 39.5 G
FAT: 18.5 G
IRON: 12.3%
HIGH IN POTASSIUM, VITAMIN A, VITAMIN B6,
    VITAMIN C, FOLATE, MAGNESIUM, MANGANESE,
    PANTOTHENIC ACID, AND RIBOFLAVIN.

Green Smoothie Joy!

Green Snack Smoothie

A LARGE HANDFUL OF LAMB'S
    LETTUCE LEAVES
2 INCHES APPROX OF
    CUCUMBER
A SMALL HANDFUL OF
    CORIANDER (CILANTRO) OR
    DANDELION LEAVES
¼ AVOCADO
1 BANANA
1 HANDFULS OF
    BLUEBERRIES
1 CUP OF WATERMELON
1 CUP OF WATER
ICE

1. Blend all ingredients until smooth.

NUTRITION:
ENERGY: 134.7 CALORIES
PROTEIN: 2.3 G
CARBS: 32.6 G
FAT: 0.8 G
IRON: 4.3%
HIGH IN POTASSIUM, VITAMIN C, MANGANESE,
    PANTOTHENIC ACID, AND THIAMINE.

Green Smoothie Joy!

Blackberry & Date Green Smoothie

1–2 CUPS OF ALMOND MILK

1   AVOCADO

A SLICE OF PINEAPPLE

A HANDFUL OF MIXED LETTUCE
    LEAVES

1   HANDFUL OF
    BLACKBERRIES

1   TBSP FLAX SEED

1   INCH OF CUCUMBER

4   DATES

A LITTLE HONEY (OPTIONAL)

ICE

1. Put all ingredients apart from the water in the blender and smooth it. Taste the smoothie and see if you need to add water to make it more runny or more almond milk if you like the taste.

NUTRITION:

ENERGY: 530.5 CALORIES

PROTEIN: 7.2 G

CARBS: 60.8 G

FAT: 32.7 G

IRON: 17.7%

HIGH IN POTASSIUM, VITAMIN A, VITAMIN B6,
    VITAMIN C, VITAMIN D, VITAMIN E, CALCIUM,
    COPPER, FOLATE, MAGNESIUM, MANGANESE,
    NIACIN, PANTOTHENIC ACID, PHOSPHORUS, AND
    RIBOFLAVIN.

Orange & Plum Green Smoothie

1 ORANGE
2 PLUMS
1 AVOCADO
1 HANDFUL OF KALE
1 MINT LEAF
1–2 CUPS OF WATER
ICE CUBES

1. Blend all ingredients in the blender adding the ice as the last step.

NUTRITION:
ENERGY: 508.8 CALORIES
PROTEIN: 11 G
CARBS: 66.4 G
FAT: 28.2 G
IRON: 21.3%
HIGH IN POTASSIUM, VITAMIN A, VITAMIN B6, VITAMIN C, VITAMIN D, VITAMIN E, CALCIUM, COPPER, FOLATE, MAGNESIUM, MANGANESE, NIACIN, PANTOTHENIC ACID, PHOSPHORUS, AND RIBOFLAVIN.

Berry & Cabbage Green Smoothie

1 CUP OF STRAWBERRIES
1 CUP OF CABBAGE – GREEN OR RED (RED MAKES A NICE BRIGHT SMOOTHIE)
1 BANANA
1 SMALL HANDFUL OF ALFALFA SPROUTS OR BEAN SPROUTS
1 AVOCADO
2 CUPS OF WATER

1. Blend all together and add some ice to keep it refreshing.

If you are worried about bloating and gas, you can juice the cabbage instead, which may help.

NUTRITION:
ENERGY: 478.8 CALORIES
PROTEIN: 8 G
CARBS: 59.5 G
FAT: 28.3 G
IRON: 15.9%
HIGH IN POTASSIUM, VITAMIN A, VITAMIN B6, VITAMIN C, VITAMIN D, VITAMIN E, CALCIUM, COPPER, FOLATE, MAGNESIUM, MANGANESE, NIACIN, PANTOTHENIC ACID, PHOSPHORUS, AND RIBOFLAVIN.

Cherry Top Green Smoothie

1-2 CUPS OF RED CHERRIES
    (PITTED)
1   CUP OF BLUEBERRIES
1   FROZEN BANANA
1   HANDFUL OF BABY SPINACH
    OR CHARD
1   TBSP OF VANILLA RICE
    PROTEIN POWDER OR OTHER
    VANILLA PROTEIN POWDER
1-2 CUPS OF WATER

1. Add all ingredients into a blender and mix until
    smooth. You can try this with hemp or almond milk
    instead of water. I suggest you de-seed the cherries
    beforehand and freeze them—that way you can
    make your smoothie quickly when you want.

NUTRITION:
DEPENDS ON THE PROTEIN POWDER INGREDIENTS.
HIGH IN POTASSIUM, VITAMIN A, VITAMIN B6,
    VITAMIN C, VITAMIN D, VITAMIN E, CALCIUM,
    COPPER, FOLATE, MAGNESIUM, MANGANESE,
    NIACIN, PANTOTHENIC ACID, PHOSPHORUS, AND
    RIBOFLAVIN.

Mango Mint Green Smoothie

½ MANGO
2 INCHES OF CUCUMBER
SEVERAL SLICES OF FROZEN
    BANANA
1 APPLE
A HANDFUL OF LAMBS LETTUCE
    AND WATERCRESS OR
    SPINACH
2 FRESH MINT LEAVES
1 CUP OF WATER
ICE

1. Blend all ingredients together until smooth. Add some ice to make it more refreshing.

NUTRITION:
ENERGY: 302.3 CALORIES
PROTEIN: 4.6 G
CARBS: 76.1 G
FAT: 1.5 G
IRON: 17.9%
HIGH IN POTASSIUM, VITAMIN A, VITAMIN B6,
    VITAMIN C, VITAMIN D, VITAMIN E, CALCIUM,
    COPPER, FOLATE, MAGNESIUM, MANGANESE,
    NIACIN, PANTOTHENIC ACID, PHOSPHORUS, AND
    RIBOFLAVIN.

Minty Berry Green Smoothie

1 CUP OF FROZEN
   RASPBERRIES
1 CUP OF STRAWBERRIES
1 FROZEN BANANA
2 MINT LEAVES
1 HANDFUL OF GREENS
   OF CHOICE OR MUSTARD
   GREENS
OPTIONAL – 1 OR 2 BRAZIL
   NUTS

1. Blend all ingredients together and add 1 mint leaf
   and taste before adding another.

NUTRITION:
ENERGY: 552.1 CALORIES
PROTEIN: 11.8 G
FAT: 6.7 G
IRON: 32.2%
HIGH IN POTASSIUM, VITAMIN A, VITAMIN B6,
   VITAMIN C, VITAMIN D, VITAMIN E, CALCIUM,
   COPPER, FOLATE, MAGNESIUM, MANGANESE,
   NIACIN, PANTOTHENIC ACID, PHOSPHORUS, AND
   RIBOFLAVIN.

Green Smoothie Joy!

Watermelon Green Smoothie

2–3 CUPS OF WATERMELON
1   ORANGE
½   BANANA
2   KALE LEAVES OR SOME
     DANDELION LEAVES
A SQUEEZE OF LEMON OR LIME
OPTIONAL HALF AN AVOCADO
OPTIONAL – A HANDFUL OF
     STRAWBERRIES
1   CUP OF WATER

1. You can juice the orange or cut it up and put it in blender along with the rest of the ingredients. Blend until smooth.

NUTRITION:
ENERGY: 827.3 CALORIES
PROTEIN: 15.7 G
CARBS: 124.4 G
FAT: 39.5 G
IRON: 28.9%
HIGH IN POTASSIUM, VITAMIN A, VITAMIN B6,
     VITAMIN C, VITAMIN D, VITAMIN E, CALCIUM,
     COPPER, FOLATE, MAGNESIUM, MANGANESE,
     NIACIN, PANTOTHENIC ACID, PHOSPHORUS, AND
     RIBOFLAVIN.

Green Smoothie Joy!

Apple & Cucumber Detox Green Smoothie

2   APPLES
½ A CUCUMBER
1   AVOCADO
A COUPLE OF SPRIGS OF
    PARSLEY
1   TSP OF HONEY

1. Mix all in a blender and add some ice for coolness.
    Parsley has a strong taste, so you may have to add
    only a small amount according to taste.

NUTRITION:
ENERGY: 396.4 CALORIES
PROTEIN: 5.2 G
CARBS: 41.3 G
FAT: 27.2 G
IRON: 15.7%
HIGH IN POTASSIUM, VITAMIN A, VITAMIN B6,
     VITAMIN C, COPPER, FOLATE, MAGNESIUM,
       MANGANESE, NIACIN, AND PANTOTHENIC ACID.

Green Smoothie Joy!

Mint Choc Chip Green Smoothie

3 MINT LEAVES
1 AVOCADO
1 TSP OF ORGANIC COCOA POWDER
1 TSP OF CACAO NIBS
1 HANDFUL OF SPINACH LEAVES
1 TSP OF VANILLA EXTRACT OR ½ A VANILLA POD (INSIDES SCRAPED OUT)
1 CUP OF COCONUT MILK OR COCONUT WATER

1. Add all ingredients to a blender and mix. If you are using a vanilla pod, add this last.

NUTRITION:
ENERGY: 375.8 CALORIES
PROTEIN: 8.8 G
CARBS: 22.4 G
FAT: 31.8 G
IRON: 51.8%
HIGH IN POTASSIUM, VITAMIN A, VITAMIN B6, VITAMIN C, COPPER, FOLATE, MAGNESIUM, MANGANESE, NIACIN, PANTOTHENIC ACID, AND PHOSPHORUS.

Green Smoothie Joy!

Parsley & Blueberry Detox Green Smoothie

1   CUP OF PARSLEY APPROX.
2   CUPS OF BLUEBERRIES
2   BANANAS
OPTIONAL – SOME MANGO
1   CUP OF WATER
SEVERAL ICE CUBES

1. Mix all ingredients together in the blender.

NUTRITION:
ENERGY: 454.7 CALORIES
PROTEIN: 6.5 G
CARBS: 114.3 G
FAT: 1.9 G
IRON: 28.1%
HIGH IN POTASSIUM, VITAMIN A, VITAMIN B6,
    VITAMIN C, VITAMIN E, FOLATE, MAGNESIUM,
        MANGANESE, THIAMINE, AND RIBOFLAVIN.

Tropical Sweet Green Smoothie

1 BANANA
A FEW CHUNKS OF PINEAPPLE
A FEW CHUNKS OF MANGO
¼ CUP OF COCONUT CREAM OR
  1 CUP OF COCONUT MILK OR
  WATER
1 HANDFUL OF KALE LEAVES
ADDITIONAL WATER IF
  NECESSARY

1. Add all ingredients to blender and blend until smooth. Test the thickness and add more water if necessary.

NUTRITION:
ENERGY: 243.9 CALORIES
PROTEIN: 4.5 G
CARBS: 58.8 G
FAT: 2.2 G
IRON: 11.1%
HIGH IN POTASSIUM, VITAMIN A, VITAMIN B6,
    VITAMIN C, VITAMIN E, CALCIUM, COPPER, AND
    MANGANESE.

Breakfast Treat Green Smoothie

½ CUP OF OATMEAL OR OATS
   (BLEND OATS DOWN FIRST)
1 BANANA
4 STRAWBERRIES
1–2 CUPS OF MILK OF CHOICE
1 HANDFUL OF SPINACH,
   COLLARD GREENS, OR
   OTHER GREENS OF CHOICE
EXTRA WATER IF LIMITING THE
   MILK CONTENT

1. Blend all ingredients until smooth.

NUTRITION:
ENERGY: 508.2 CALORIES
PROTEIN: 23.9 G
CARBS: 110.3 G
FAT: 8.3 G
IRON: 29.4%
HIGH IN POTASSIUM, VITAMIN A, B VITAMINS,
   VITAMIN C, VITAMIN D, CALCIUM, COPPER,
   FOLATE, MAGNESIUM, MANGANESE, NIACIN,
   PANTOTHENIC ACID, SELENIUM, ZINC, THIAMINE,
   PHOSPHORUS, AND RIBOFLAVIN.

Cinnamon Treat Green Smoothie

1   FROZEN BANANA
1   SMALL CARROT
1   APPLE
1   TSP OF CINNAMON
1   HANDFUL OF BABY SPINACH
1   CUP OF WATER
ICE
A LITTLE HONEY

1. Blend all ingredients together until smooth.

NUTRITION:
ENERGY: 221.9 CALORIES
PROTEIN: 2.8 G
CARBS: 55.7 G
FAT: 1.1 G
IRON: 9.0%
HIGH IN POTASSIUM, VITAMIN A, VITAMIN B6,
        VITAMIN C, FOLATE, AND MANGANESE.

Green Smoothie Joy!

Tomato Cream Green Smoothie

2 TOMATOES
SEVERAL CHUNKS OF
   WATERMELON
½ AVOCADO
A HANDFUL OF CILANTRO OR
   CORIANDER
½ STICK OF CELERY
A SQUEEZE OF LEMON
1 CUP OF WATER
ICE

1. Blend all ingredients until smooth.

NUTRITION:
ENERGY: 251.9 CALORIES
PROTEIN: 5.3 G
CARBS: 31.8 G
FAT: 5.0 G
IRON: 12.9%
HIGH IN POTASSIUM, VITAMIN A, VITAMIN B6,
   VITAMIN C, FOLATE, MANGANESE, AND
      PANTOTHENIC ACID.

Dandelion & Apple Green Smoothie

2 SQUEEZES OF LEMON

1 BUNCH OF DANDELION GREENS OR GREENS OF CHOICE

2 APPLES

1 LARGE BANANA

1 TBSP OF MILLED CHIA SEED

1 CUP OF WATER APPROX

1. Put in all the ingredients into the blender and blend—add some ice to make it refreshing.

NUTRITION:

ENERGY: 401.3 CALORIES

PROTEIN: 3.5 G

CARBS: 2.4 G

FAT: 1.6 G

IRON: 11.9%

HIGH IN POTASSIUM, VITAMIN A, VITAMIN B6, VITAMIN C, FOLATE, AND MANGANESE.

Green Smoothie Joy!

Blackberry Burst Green Smoothie

2   LARGE LETTUCE LEAVES
1   WHOLE ORANGE
    (DE-SEEDED AND WITHOUT
    PITH IF POSSIBLE)
1   CUP OF BLACKBERRIES
A HANDFUL OF SPINACH OR
    KALE
SOME ZEST OF AN ORANGE
    (GRATED PEEL)
1   BANANA
ICE
1   CUP OF WATER

1. Mix all ingredients in a blender until smooth.

NUTRITION:
ENERGY: 309.1 CALORIES
PROTEIN: 6.7 G
CARBS: 75.6 G
FAT: 2.0 G
IRON: 15.4%
HIGH IN POTASSIUM, VITAMIN A, VITAMIN B6,
    VITAMIN C, CALCIUM, COPPER, FOLATE,
    MAGNESIUM, AND MANGANESE.

Blackberry Blue Green Smoothie

2   HANDFULS OF SWISS
    CHARD
1   CUP OF BLUEBERRIES
1   CUP OF BLACKBERRIES
1   FROZEN BANANA
1   CUP OF WATER

1. Mix all ingredients in a blender until smooth.

NUTRITION:
ENERGY: 27.6 CALORIES
PROTEIN: 4.0 G
CARBS: 67.8 G
FAT: 1.3 G
IRON: 11.1%
HIGH IN POTASSIUM, VITAMIN A, VITAMIN B6,
    VITAMIN C, FOLATE, AND MANGANESE.

Green Smoothie Joy!

Choco Peach Green Smoothie

2 BANANAS
1 PEACH
A HANDFUL OF RASPBERRIES
2 HANDFULS SPINACH
2 TSP CACAO
1 TSP MACA
WATER

1. Blend all ingredients until smooth.

NUTRITION:
ENERGY: 364.2 CALORIES
PROTEIN: 6.4 G
CARBS: 90.7 G
FAT: 2.3 G
IRON: 18.0%
HIGH IN POTASSIUM, VITAMIN A, VITAMIN B6,
    VITAMIN C, COPPER, FOLATE, MAGNESIUM,
        MANGANESE, NIACIN, AND RIBOFLAVIN.

Berry Basil Green Smoothie

2 CUPS OF FROZEN MIXED
  BERRIES
A SMALL HANDFUL OF BASIL
  LEAVES
1 CUP OF WATER
1 TBSP OF COCONUT CREAM
(OR YOU CAN JUST USE 1 CUP
  OF COCONUT MILK OR
  WATER)
1 TBSP OF FLAX SEED OR
  PUMPKIN SEED

1. Put all ingredients into a blender and smooth it.

NUTRITION:
ENERGY: 157.5 CALORIES
PROTEIN: 3.0 G
CARBS: 36.0 G
FAT: 1.7 G
IRON: 13.6%
  HIGH IN POTASSIUM, VITAMIN C, AND MANGANESE.

Blackberry & Seed Green Smoothie

1 FROZEN BANANA

1 HANDFUL OF BLACKBERRIES

1 HANDFUL OF BABY SPINACH LEAVES

A SPRINKLE OF SEEDS OF CHOICE

1 TBSP OF VANILLA RICE PROTEIN (OR OTHER VANILLA-FLAVORED PROTEIN POWDER)

1 CUP OF OAT MILK OR OTHER NON-DAIRY UNSWEETENED MILK ALTERNATIVE

1. Blend all together until smooth. If using pumpkin seeds, remember to soak them overnight to release their enzymes.

NUTRITION:
ENERGY: 250.3 CALORIES
PROTEIN: 4.0 G
CARBS: 55.2 G
FAT: 3.8 G
IRON: 13.1%
HIGH IN POTASSIUM, VITAMIN A, VITAMIN B6, VITAMIN C, VITAMIN D, VITAMIN E, CALCIUM, FOLATE, AND MANGANESE.

Green Smoothie Joy!

Juice It,
Smooth It Recipes

Hot Green Smoothie

1 CUP CARROT JUICE
½ CUP OF CELERY JUICE
½ CUP OF CUCUMBER JUICE
1 TSP HOT SAUCE
1 TSP LEMON JUICE
1 HANDFUL OF SPINACH
  LEAVES
SMALL HANDFUL OF PARSLEY
  LEAVES
1 CUP OF ICE CUBES

1. Juice about 3 or 4 large carrots, a stick of celery, and half a cucumber.

2. Pour into the blender.

3. Add the rest of the ingredients and blend until creamy. Add an avocado for a more creamy texture.

NUTRITION:
ENERGY: 87.7 CALORIES
PROTEIN: 4.2 G
CARBS: 18.6 G
FAT: 1.0 G
IRON: 28.1%
HIGH IN POTASSIUM, VITAMIN A, VITAMIN C, FOLATE,
    AND MANGANESE.

Pomegranate Green Smoothie

1   CUP OF BLUEBERRIES

A FEW DRIED GOJI BERRIES

½   CUP FRESH POMEGRANATE
    JUICE (JUICE FROM
    2 POMEGRANATES)

1   MEDIUM BANANA

2   HANDFULS OF LAMB'S
    LETTUCE

2   CUPS OF WATER

SOME ICE

1. Juice the pomegranates.

2. Blend with the other ingredients.

NUTRITION:
ENERGY: 226.7 CALORIES
PROTEIN: 3.3 G
CARBS: 57.1 G
FAT: 0.8 G
IRON: 6.6%
HIGH IN POTASSIUM, VITAMIN A, VITAMIN B6,
       VITAMIN C, FOLATE, AND MANGANESE.

Morning Wake Up Green Smoothie

HALF A CUP OF CUCUMBER
JUICE (ABOUT HALF A
CUCUMBER)

1 HANDFUL OF SPINACH OR
KALE

½ AVOCADO

1 TBSP OF RICE PROTEIN
POWDER (OR OTHER)

2 HANDFULS OF
RASPBERRIES

1 CUP OF WATER
APPROX

1. Juice the cucumber then add to the blender. Fill
   with other ingredients plus water and blend until
   smooth.

NUTRITION:
ENERGY: 283.6 CALORIES
PROTEIN: 5.4 G
CARBS: 39.5 G
FAT: 14.9 G
IRON: 16.5%
HIGH IN POTASSIUM, VITAMIN A, VITAMIN B6,
    VITAMIN C, FOLATE, MAGNESIUM, MANGANESE,
        NIACIN, PANTOTHENIC ACID, AND RIBOFLAVIN.

Lunchtime Survival Green Smoothie

JUICE OF 2–3 FLORETS OF
    BROCCOLI (HALF A LARGE
    HEAD)
1 OR 2 STICKS WORTH OF
    CELERY JUICE
SEVERAL CHUNKS PINEAPPLE
1   AVOCADO
½   BANANA
A FEW STRAWBERRIES
HANDFUL OF SPINACH LEAVES
A COUPLE OF ICE CUBES
EXTRA WATER IF NECESSARY

1. Juice the broccoli and celery and add to blender.
    Add the other ingredients and smooth it.

NUTRITION:
ENERGY: 448.8 CALORIES
PROTEIN: 6.2 G
CARBS: 54.5 G
FAT: 27.9 G
IRON: 15.6%
HIGH IN POTASSIUM, VITAMIN A, VITAMIN B6,
    VITAMIN C, COPPER, FOLATE, MAGNESIUM,
    MANGANESE, NIACIN, PANTOTHENIC ACID,
    THIAMINE, AND RIBOFLAVIN.

Chocolate Blueberry Green Smoothie

1 TBSP OF CACAO NIBS OR ORGANIC DARK CHOCOLATE POWDER
½ CUP OF CARROT JUICE
1 BANANA
1 CUP OF BLUEBERRIES
2 HANDFULS OF SPINACH LEAVES
2 CUPS OF WATER

1. Juice about 2 or 3 carrots. Blend with all the other ingredients until smooth.

2. Add some ice to cool it.

NUTRITION:
ENERGY: 295.2 CALORIES
PROTEIN: 5 G
CARBS: 73.3 G
FAT: 0.9 G
IRON: 14.3%
HIGH IN POTASSIUM, VITAMIN A, VITAMIN B6,
    VITAMIN C, VITAMIN E, FOLATE, MANGANESE,
    AND RIBOFLAVIN.

Blackberry & Apple Crunch Green Smoothie

1 CUP OF BLACKBERRIES
JUICE OF 1 APPLE
1 SMALL AVOCADO
4 LEAVES OF ROMAINE
   LETTUCE
A FEW ALMONDS OR BRAZIL
   NUTS
2 CUPS OF WATER APPROX
SEVERAL ICE CUBES

1. Juice the cucumber and apple. Add to blender with other ingredients and smooth it—add the ice last and blend again. The almonds may blend down until smooth, otherwise you will have a slightly crunchy smoothie!

NUTRITION:
ENERGY: 426.3 CALORIES
PROTEIN: 6.1 G
CARBS: 42.5 G
FAT: 29.8 G
IRON: 15.3%
HIGH IN POTASSIUM, VITAMIN A, VITAMIN B6,
   VITAMIN C, VITAMIN E, COPPER, FOLATE,
   MAGNESIUM, MANGANESE, NIACIN,
   PANTOTHENIC ACID, PHOSPHORUS, AND
   RIBOFLAVIN.

Broccoli Boost Green Smoothie

2–3 BROCCOLI FLORETS –
   JUICED
1 PEAR
1 APPLE
1 AVOCADO
SOME WATER
A FEW ICE CUBES

1. Juice the broccoli and add to the blender. Mix all the other ingredients together in the blender and smooth with the ice.

NUTRITION:
ENERGY: 475.7 CALORIES
PROTEIN: 5.0 G
CARBS: 62.5 G
FAT: 27.6 G
IRON: 10.9%
HIGH IN POTASSIUM, VITAMIN B6, VITAMIN C,
   VITAMIN E, COPPER, FOLATE, MANGANESE, AND
      PANTOTHENIC ACID.

Green Smoothie Joy!

Passion Fruit Experience Green Smoothie

2   PASSION FRUIT
1   HANDFUL OF
    STRAWBERRIES
½   A MANGO
1   HANDFUL OF CORIANDER OR
    CILANTRO
THE JUICE OF 2 INCHES OF
    CUCUMBER
1   CUP OF WATER
ICE

1. Juice the cucumber and add to blender with remaining ingredients.

2. Add a sprig of mint for garnish?

3. Add a squeeze of lime juice?

NUTRITION:
ENERGY: 205.9 CALORIES
PROTEIN: 3.5 G
CARBS: 51.1 G
FAT: 1.6 G
IRON: 9.6%
HIGH IN POTASSIUM, VITAMIN A, VITAMIN C, COPPER,
    FOLATE, AND MANGANESE.

Apple & Pear Power Green Smoothie

JUICE OF 1 APPLE
JUICE OF 1 PEAR
1   AVOCADO
A HANDFUL OF BABY SPINACH
1   TSP OF GREEN SUPERFOOD
    POWDER OF CHOICE

1. Juice the apple and pear. Add to the blender with the rest of the ingredients and smooth it.

NUTRITION:
ENERGY: 371.8 CALORIES
PROTEIN: 4.6 G
CARBS: 35.2 G
FAT: 27.1 G
IRON: 12.9%
HIGH IN POTASSIUM, VITAMIN A, VITAMIN B6,
    VITAMIN C, FOLATE, MANGANESE, PANTOTHENIC
        ACID, AND RIBOFLAVIN.

Kiwi Paradise Green Smoothie

JUICE OF 1 APPLE

2 KIWI FRUIT

1 HANDFUL OF SWISS CHARD

½ AN AVOCADO

A SQUEEZE OF LIME

2 MINT LEAVES (OPTIONAL)

1 CUP OF WATER

ICE

1. Juice the apple and add to the blender. Add all other ingredients and blend.

NUTRITION:

ENERGY: 277.7 CALORIES

PROTEIN: 3.9 G

CARBS: 39.7 G

FAT: 14.2 G

IRON: 10.4%

HIGH IN POTASSIUM, VITAMIN A, VITAMIN B6, VITAMIN C, COPPER, FOLATE, AND MANGANESE.

Green Smoothie Joy!

Beet It Green Smoothie

JUICE OF 1 RAW BEETROOT

1   APPLE

½   AN AVOCADO

1   HANDFUL OF LETTUCE OF CHOICE

1   SQUEEZE OF LEMON

1   TSP OF CACAO NIBS

1   TSP OF MILLED CHIA SEEDS

1   CUP OF WATER

ICE

1. Juice the beetroot and add to the blender. Add the other ingredients to the blender and smooth with the ice.

NUTRITION:

ENERGY: 244.5 CALORIES

PROTEIN: 2.9 G

CARBS: 32.5 G

FAT: 3.7 G

IRON: 7.6%

HIGH IN POTASSIUM, VITAMIN C, FOLATE, AND MANGANESE.

Green Smoothie Joy!

Fennel Fantastic Green Smoothie

JUICE OF ½ A FENNEL BULB
(YOU CAN CHOP THE STALKS
AND LEAVES AND ADD TO
THE SMOOTHIE IF YOU WISH)
½ AN ORANGE
JUICE OF ½ A LIME
½ AN AVOCADO
½ A BANANA
2 OR 3 MINT LEAVES
1 CUP OF WATER
ICE

1. Juice the fennel and lime and add to the blender and mix with the other ingredients.

NUTRITION:
ENERGY: 286.9 CALORIES
PROTEIN: 4.2 G
CARBS: 44.5 G
FAT: 14.0 G
IRON: 7.8%
HIGH IN POTASSIUM, VITAMIN B6, VITAMIN C, AND
FOLATE.

Green Smoothie Joy!

Brussel Sprout Green Smoothie

JUICE OF 2 BRUSSEL SPROUTS
JUICE OF ¼ CUCUMBER
JUICE OF 2 APPLES
1   AVOCADO
A SQUEEZE OF LEMON
ICE

1. Juice the apples and brussel sprouts. Add to the blender with the other ingredients. Smooth it.

NUTRITION:
ENERGY: 334.0 CALORIES
PROTEIN: 4.1 G
CARBS: 25.6 G
FAT: 26.9 G
IRON: 9.0%
HIGH IN POTASSIUM, VITAMIN B6, VITAMIN C, FOLATE,
     AND PANTOTHENIC ACID.

Quick Cold Fix Green Smoothie

JUICE OF 1 ORANGE (OR YOU
   CAN BLEND AN ORANGE IF
   YOU PREFER)
A HANDFUL OF RASPBERRIES
1   KIWI FRUIT
A LONG SQUEEZE OF LEMON
1   TSP OF GREEN BARLEY
   GRASS OR OTHER GREEN
   SUPERFOOD
1   BANANA
1   TSP OF HONEY

1. Juice the orange. Combine in blender with other ingredients.

NUTRITION:
ENERGY: 311.9 CALORIES
PROTEIN: 3.7 G
CARBS: 78.1 G
FAT: 1.8 G
IRON: 8.9%
HIGH IN POTASSIUM, VITAMIN B6, VITAMIN C,
      FOLATE, MAGNESIUM, AND MANGANESE.

Body Boosting Green Smoothie

1 SMALL JUICED RAW
  BEETROOT
1 JUICED CARROT
1 JUICED STICK OF CELERY
1 AVOCADO
1 HANDFUL OF BABY SPINACH
  LEAVES
1 HANDFUL OF BLUEBERRIES
1 CUP OF WATER
ICE

1. Juice the beet, carrot, and celery. Add to blender with the other ingredients.

NUTRITION:
ENERGY: 393.7 CALORIES
PROTEIN: 5.8 G
CARBS: 40.4 G
FAT: 26.9 G
IRON: 13.1%
HIGH IN POTASSIUM, VITAMIN A, VITAMIN B6,
    VITAMIN C, VITAMIN E, COPPER, FOLATE,
    MAGNESIUM, MANGANESE, NIACIN,
       PANTOTHENIC ACID, AND RIBOFLAVIN.

Green Smoothie Joy!

Apple & Lemon Green Smoothie

2   HANDFULS OF SPRING
    GREENS
SQUEEZE FROM HALF A LEMON
2   APPLES-JUICED
½   AVOCADO
½   BANANA
1   CUP OF WATER APPROX
ICE

1. Juice the apples and lemon (or you can just squeeze).

2. Blend all ingredients together in blender until smooth.

NUTRITION:
ENERGY: 234.2 CALORIES
PROTEIN: 2.7 G
CARBS: 31.8 G
FAT: 13.8 G
IRON: 4.4%
HIGH IN POTASSIUM, VITAMIN B6, VITAMIN C, AND
    FOLATE.

Green Smoothie Joy!

Apple & Carrot Green Smoothie

JUICE OF 2 APPLES
JUICE OF 2 CARROTS
JUICE OF 2 CELERY STICKS
1   AVOCADO
½   CUCUMBER
DASH OF LEMON
SOME ICE

1. Juice the apples, carrot, and celery. Add to the blender with the other ingredients. Blend with the ice.

NUTRITION:
ENERGY: 444.6 CALORIES
PROTEIN: 5.2 G
CARBS: 52.6 G
FAT: 27.3 G
IRON: 14.6%
HIGH IN POTASSIUM, VITAMIN A, VITAMIN B6,
    VITAMIN C, FOLATE, MAGNESIUM, MANGANESE,
    NIACIN, PANTOTHENIC ACID, AND RIBOFLAVIN.

Some Fruity, Some Yogurty Smoothies

Apple & Melon Smoothie

2   CUPS OF HONEYDEW
    MELON, CUT INTO PIECES
1   APPLE
2   TBSP OF ORGANIC LIVE
    YOGURT (GREEK YOGURT IS
    NICE AND THICK)
1   TBSP LIME JUICE
1   CUP OF WATER
ICE CUBES

1. Place all the ingredients into the blender and
    smooth it.

NUTRITION:
ENERGY: 291.2 CALORIES
PROTEIN: 5.5 G
CARBS: 68.9 G
FAT: 1.8 G
IRON: 5.8%
HIGH IN POTASSIUM, VITAMIN B6, VITAMIN C, AND
       FOLATE.

Sweet Pear Smoothie

1   PEAR (CORED)
1   BANANA, CUT INTO SMALL
    CHUNKS
1   TSP HONEY
1   CUP OF ALMOND MILK
6   ICE CUBES

1. Blend all together until smooth.

NUTRITION:
ENERGY: 330.3 CALORIES
PROTEIN: 2.9 G
CARBS: 78.1 G
FAT: 3.8 G
IRON: 6.8%
HIGH IN POTASSIUM, VITAMIN B6, VITAMIN C,
        VITAMIN D, VITAMIN E, AND CALCIUM.

Papaya Strawberry Smoothie

1 PAPAYA, PEELED AND DICED
½ FROZEN BANANA
1 SLICE OF PINEAPPLE
1 HANDFUL OF
  STRAWBERRIES
1 CUP OF WATER
ICE

1. Blend all ingredients and then add the ice.

NUTRITION:
ENERGY: 309.5 CALORIES
PROTEIN: 4.3 G
CARBS: 77.4 G
FAT: 1.9 G
IRON: 8.4%
HIGH IN POTASSIUM, VITAMIN A, VITAMIN B6,
        VITAMIN C, FOLATE, AND MANGANESE.

Green Smoothie Joy!

Strawberry Grapefruit Detoxifying Smoothie

½ A GRAPEFRUIT
1 HANDFUL OF RASPBERRIES
1 BANANA
OPTIONAL – ADD LIVE YOGURT
    FOR AN EVEN CREAMIER
    TEXTURE
1 CUP OF WATER APPROX
ICE

1. Blend all ingredients until smooth. Add a little water first and then check consistency before adding the full cup.

NUTRITION:
ENERGY: 244.3 CALORIES
PROTEIN: 6.2 G
CARBS: 55.5 G
FAT: 2.4 G
IRON: 7.0%
HIGH IN POTASSIUM, VITAMIN B6, VITAMIN C,
    MANGANESE, AND RIBOFLAVIN.

Green Smoothie Joy!

Cherry Berry Smoothie

2 CUPS OF CHERRIES (PITTED)
1   BANANA
1   CUP OF RASPBERRIES
1   APPLE
OPTIONAL – DARK CHOCOLATE
    CHUNKS OR 1–2 TSP OF
    COCOA POWDER OR CACAO
    NIBS
1   CUP OF WATER
ICE

1. Blend all the ingredients along with the ice and a little water. Add more water if you need it.

NUTRITION:
ENERGY: 482.6 CALORIES
PROTEIN: 5.7 G
CARBS: 120.0 G
FAT: 2.7 G
IRON: 14.6%
HIGH IN POTASSIUM, VITAMIN B6, VITAMIN C,
    COPPER, MAGNESIUM, MANGANESE, AND
        RIBOFLAVIN.

Pom Berry Smoothie

1 CUP OF STRAWBERRIES
JUICE OF 1 OR 2
  POMEGRANATES
1 BANANA
1 CUP OF RASPBERRIES
1 CUP OF WATER OR ALMOND
  MILK
ICE

1. Juice the pomegranates and then place all the ingredients in the blender and mix until smooth.

NUTRITION:
ENERGY: 295.3 CALORIES
PROTEIN: 4.5 G
CARBS: 65.9 G
FAT: 4.5 G
IRON: 11.6%
HIGH IN POTASSIUM, VITAMIN B6, VITAMIN C.
  VITAMIN D, VITAMIN E, CALCIUM, FOLATE.
    MAGNESIUM, MANGANESE, AND RIBOFLAVIN.

Green Smoothie Joy!

Coco Mango Smoothie

1   MANGO
1   BANANA
2   SLICES OF PINEAPPLE
    JUICED
1   TBSP OF COCONUT CREAM
    OR 1 CUP OF COCONUT MILK
    OR WATER
WATER
ICE

1. Just put the ingredients into the blender and whizz it!

2. Great for a quick fruit blast.

NUTRITION:
ENERGY: 385.5 CALORIES
PROTEIN: 3.9 G
CARBS: 9.7 G
FAT: 4.4 G
IRON: 9.0%
HIGH IN POTASSIUM, VITAMIN A, VITAMIN B6,
    VITAMIN C, VITAMIN D, VITAMIN E, CALCIUM,
    COPPER, MANGANESE, AND THIAMINE.

Green Smoothie Joy!

Peach & Almond Smoothie

2 SLICES OF PINEAPPLE

1 BANANA

2 TBSP SWEET ALMONDS OR
    PECANS

1 PEACH, PITTED

½ AN AVOCADO

WATER

1. Blend all together in the blender.

NUTRITION:

ENERGY: 624.7 CALORIES

PROTEIN: 13.3 G

CARBS: 74.9 G

FAT: 36.7 G

IRON: 19.4%

HIGH IN POTASSIUM, VITAMIN B6, VITAMIN C,
    VITAMIN E, COPPER, FOLATE, MAGNESIUM,
    MANGANESE, NIACIN, PANTOTHENIC ACID,
    PHOSPHORUS, THIAMIN, AND RIBOFLAVIN.

Green Smoothie Joy!

Blueberry Nut Smoothie

1   PEACH
1   CUP OF BLUEBERRIES
1   CUP OF WATER
2   BRAZIL NUTS OR OTHER
¼   TSP VANILLA EXTRACT
ICE

1. Combine all ingredients in the blender and smooth it.

NUTRITION:
ENERGY: 140.3 CALORIES
PROTEIN: 2.3 G
CARBS: 31.9 G
FAT: 1.6 G
IRON: 2.7%
HIGH IN POTASSIUM, VITAMIN C, VITAMIN E, AND
      MANGANESE.

Pineapple & Nectarine Energy Smoothie

1 BANANA, PEELED AND CUT
   IN CHUNKS
2 NECTARINES, PEELED,
   PITTED, AND CUT IN CHUNKS
2 SLICES OF PINEAPPLE
1 CUP OF WATER OR MILK
1 TBSP OF PROTEIN POWDER
   (VANILLA RICE PROTEIN)
SOME WATER AND ICE AS
   REQUIRED

1. Place all the ingredients into the blender and blend
    until smooth.

NUTRITION:
ENERGY: 420.6 CALORIES
PROTEIN: 12.9 G
CARBS: 89.4 G
FAT: 4.7 G
IRON: 10.1%
HIGH IN POTASSIUM, VITAMIN A, B VITAMINS,
    VITAMIN C, VITAMIN D, CALCIUM, COPPER,
    MANGANESE, NIACIN, PANTOTHENIC ACID,
        PHOSPHORUS, THIAMINE, AND RIBOFLAVIN.

Green Smoothie Joy!

Melon Berry Yogurt Smoothie

½ OF A CANTALOUPE MELON
1 CUP OF STRAWBERRIES
½ BANANA
1 CUP OF LIVE (HEALTHY BACTERIA INCLUDED) YOGURT

1. Mix all together in blender.

NUTRITION:
ENERGY: 428.9 CALORIES
PROTEIN: 18.5 G
CARBS: 83.8 G
FAT: 6.1 G
IRON: 10.9%
HIGH IN POTASSIUM, VITAMIN A, B VITAMINS, VITAMIN C, CALCIUM, COPPER, FOLATE, MAGNESIUM, MANGANESE, PANTOTHENIC ACID, PHOSPHORUS, THIAMINE, ZINC, AND RIBOFLAVIN.

Green Smoothie Joy!

Passion & Mango Smoothie

1 MANGO
1 CUP OF FRESH PINEAPPLE
   JUICE
3 PASSION FRUITS
1 FROZEN BANANA

1. Smooth all the ingredients in a blender and serve with ice.

NUTRITION:
ENERGY: 665.8 CALORIES
PROTEIN: 5.7 G
CARBS: 168.2 G
FAT: 2.4 G
IRON: 13.6%
HIGH IN POTASSIUM, VITAMIN A, VITAMIN B6,
    VITAMIN C, VITAMIN E, COPPER, FOLATE,
    MAGNESIUM, MANGANESE, NIACIN, RIBOFLAVIN,
    AND NIACIN.

Fill Up and Go Green Smoothies

Fruity Punch Smoothie

1 TBSP OF PROTEIN POWDER
1 HANDFUL OF SPINACH
1 SLICE OF PINEAPPLE
1 HANDFUL OF
   STRAWBERRIES
1 BANANA
1 NECTARINE
1 TSP OF FLAX SEED
1 CUP OF WATER APPROX
ICE

1. Blend all together and add ice for a cool smoothie.

NUTRITION:
ENERGY: 255 CALORIES
PROTEIN: 15.3 G
CARBS: 63.6 G
FAT: 1.7 G
IRON: 15.0%
HIGH IN POTASSIUM, VITAMIN A, VITAMIN B6,
    VITAMIN C, COPPER, FOLATE, MAGNESIUM, AND
        MANGANESE.

Chocolate Boost Green Smoothie

1 HANDFUL OF BLUEBERRIES
1 HANDFUL OF BABY LEAF GREENS
1 LARGE ROMAINE LETTUCE LEAF
1 BANANA
1 TSP OF RICE PROTEIN
1 TSP OF MACA
1 TSP OF CACAO POWDER, NIBS, OR ORGANIC DARK COCOA POWDER
1 CUP OF ALMOND MILK OR OTHER MILK OF CHOICE
ICE

1. Blend all ingredients together and add some ice at the end.

NUTRITION:
ENERGY: 255.3 CALORIES
PROTEIN: 3.8 G
CARBS: 57.2 G
FAT: 3.2 G
IRON: 7.9%
HIGH IN POTASSIUM, VITAMIN A, VITAMIN B6, VITAMIN C, VITAMIN D, VITAMIN E, CALCIUM, FOLATE, AND MANGANESE.

Wintry Green Smoothie

1 BANANA
2 CUPS OF FROZEN BERRIES
½ AN ORANGE
A HANDFUL OF SPINACH OR
   KALE
EXTRA WATER

1. Mix all in the blender until smooth. Add water as necessary. If too sweet, add a little squeeze of lemon.

NUTRITION:
ENERGY: 310.6 CALORIES
PROTEIN: 6.8 G
CARBS: 74.8 G
FAT: 2.6 G
IRON: 16.8%
HIGH IN POTASSIUM, VITAMIN A, VITAMIN B6,
    VITAMIN C, COPPER, FOLATE, MAGNESIUM,
        MANGANESE, AND RIBOFLAVIN.

Green Smoothie Joy!

Grapefruit & Pineapple Diet Yogurt Smoothie

SEVERAL CHUNKS OF
   PINEAPPLE
1 SMALL AVOCADO
A FEW LEAVES OF LETTUCE
½ A GRAPEFRUIT
A BIG SQUEEZE OF LIME
1 CUP OF LOW-FAT LIVE
   YOGURT
WATER TO MAKE LESS THICK IF
   NECESSARY

1. Blend all ingredients until smooth.

NUTRITION:
ENERGY: 560.4 CALORIES
PROTEIN: 18.0 G
CARBS: 61.3 G
FAT: 31.3 G
IRON: 12.8%
HIGH IN POTASSIUM, VITAMIN A, B VITAMINS,
   VITAMIN C, CALCIUM, COPPER, FOLATE,
   MAGNESIUM, MANGANESE, NIACIN,
   PANTOTHENIC ACID, PHOSPHORUS, THIAMINE,
      ZINC, AND RIBOFLAVIN.

Cocoa Banana Smoothie

2   RIPE BANANAS
A HANDFUL OF FROZEN
      BERRIES MIX
1   TBSP OF COCOA POWDER OR
      RAW CACAO POWDER
1   TSP OF GREEN SUPERFOOD
1   TSP OF MACA ROOT POWDER
COCONUT WATER OR CREAM
      AND ADD WATER (OR 1 CUP
      OF ALMOND MILK)
1   TSP OF MANUKA HONEY
ICE IF YOU WANT IT EXTRA COLD

1. Mix all together and blend away!

NUTRITION:
ENERGY: 321.1 CALORIES
PROTEIN: 4.4 G
CARBS: 79.0 G
FAT: 2.8 G
IRON: 14.0%
HIGH IN POTASSIUM, VITAMIN B6, VITAMIN C,
      COPPER, FOLATE, MAGNESIUM, MANGANESE,
          AND RIBOFLAVIN.

Strawberry Cream Green Smoothie

2 HANDFULS OF STRAWBERRIES

2 BANANAS

1 HANDFUL OF BABY SPINACH LEAVES

A SMALL HANDFUL OF GOJI BERRIES (SOAKED BEFOREHAND FOR APPROX 5 MINUTES)

1 TSP OF VANILLA EXTRACT (OPTIONAL)

1 CUP OF MILK OF CHOICE (COW'S, OAT, RICE, COCONUT, ETC.)

ICE

1. Blend the mixture until it is smooth. Garnish with a couple of blueberries.

NUTRITION:
ENERGY: 452.2 CALORIES
PROTEIN: 13.2 G
CARBS: 90.1 G
FAT: 5.0 G
IRON: 15.4%
HIGH IN POTASSIUM, VITAMIN A, VITAMIN B6, VITAMIN C, VITAMIN D, CALCIUM, COPPER, FOLATE, MAGNESIUM, MANGANESE, PANTOTHENIC ACID, PHOSPHORUS, AND RIBOFLAVIN.

Green Smoothie Joy!

Coffee & Almond Breakfast Smoothie

1   CUP OF COOLED BLACK
    COFFEE
A HANDFUL OF ALMONDS OR ½
    CUP OF ALMOND MILK
2   BANANAS
1   HANDFUL OF BLUEBERRIES
1   TSP HONEY
A SPRINKLE OF CINNAMON
1   HANDFUL OF SPINACH
    LEAVES
A DASH OF MILK (OPTIONAL)

1. Mix everything in a blender.

NUTRITION:
ENERGY: 411.6 CALORIES
PROTEIN: 8.3 G
CARBS: 80.6 G
FAT: 10.5 G
IRON: 14.4%
HIGH IN POTASSIUM, VITAMIN A, VITAMIN B6,
    VITAMIN C, VITAMIN E, COPPER, FOLATE,
    MAGNESIUM, MANGANESE, RIBOFLAVIN, AND
    THIAMINE.

Green Smoothie Joy!

Salad Smoothie

1 AVOCADO (OR YOU CAN USE
   2 CUPS OF YOGURT INSTEAD)
1 CUCUMBER
1 TOMATO
A SMALL BUNCH OF CHIVES
A HANDFUL OF CILANTRO OR
   CORIANDER
1 STALK OF CELERY
3 ROMAINE LETTUCE LEAVES
SALT AND PEPPER (OPTIONAL)
WATER IF NECESSARY TO MAKE
   IT LESS THICK
ICE

1. Mix all together in a blender and whizz until smooth.

NUTRITION:
ENERGY: 338.6 CALORIES
PROTEIN: 6.3 G
CARBS: 25.4 G
FAT: 27.2 G
IRON: 12.9%
HIGH IN POTASSIUM, VITAMIN A, VITAMIN B6,
   VITAMIN C, COPPER, FOLATE, MAGNESIUM,
   MANGANESE, NIACIN, PANTOTHENIC ACID,
   PHOSPHORUS, AND RIBOFLAVIN.

Green Smoothie Joy!

Time Crunched Smoothies

Fast Recipe Ideas

Strawberry Orange Smoothie

Make this with strawberries, a little honey, a banana, and an orange or orange juice.

Quick Blueberry Smoothie

Use blueberries, yogurt, or avocado, and banana.

Taste the Tropics Smoothie

Blend banana, mango, pineapple, kiwi, and an orange.

Berry Smoothie

Blend your frozen berries with yogurt or banana and milk (or water).

Pina Colada Smoothie

Blend pineapple, coconut cream, and water or coconut water, with banana.

Add a tablespoon of seeds with any of these

Such as sunflower, chia, etc. If you are adding unmilled seeds you may not get them to blend very well and you will have to drink your smoothie without a straw and with a definite crunch.

Very Sweet Naughty Smoothies

Creamy Peanut Butter Berry Smoothie

1 BANANA
1 CUP OF MIXED FROZEN
  BERRIES
½ CUP OF CREAM
2 CUPS OF WATER
1 TBSP OF PEANUT BUTTER
  (UNSWEETENED)
1 TSP OF COCOA POWDER OR
  CACAO POWDER
2 TSP MAPLE SYRUP OR
  AGAVE SYRUP

1. Place the banana and strawberry chunks into the blender. Pour in the water and cream then the rest of the ingredients.

2. Blend until smooth.

NUTRITION:
ENERGY: 698.1 CALORIES
PROTEIN: 19.1 G
CARBS: 92.4 G
FAT: 33.2 G
IRON: 11.2%
HIGH IN POTASSIUM, VITAMIN B6, VITAMIN C,
    VITAMIN E, CALCIUM, COPPER, MAGNESIUM,
    MANGANESE, NIACIN, PHOSPHORUS, ZINC, AND
    RIBOFLAVIN.

Jam Smoothie

1   CUP UNSWEETENED
    VANILLA YOGURT OR PLAIN
    YOGURT AND VANILLA
    EXTRACT
1/2 TO 1 BANANA
2   CUPS OF RASPBERRIES
1   TBSP OF NATURALLY
    SWEETENED JAM
2 CUPS OF WATER

1. Blend all until smooth and creamy.

NUTRITION:
ENERGY: 538.5 CALORIES
PROTEIN: 7.5 G
CARBS: 130.3 G
FAT: 4.5 G
IRON: 10.8%
HIGH IN POTASSIUM, VITAMIN B2, VITAMIN C,
    VITAMIN E, CALCIUM, COPPER, FOLATE,
    MAGNESIUM, MANGANESE, NIACIN,
    PANTOTHENIC ACID, ZINC, THIAMINE, AND
        RIBOFLAVIN.

Green Smoothie Joy!

Pomegranate & Strawberries Smoothie

½ CUP OF FRESH
   POMEGRANATE JUICE
1 BANANA
A HANDFUL OF STRAWBERRIES
   (OR MIXED FROZEN BERRIES)
1 LARGE TBSP OF CRÈME
   FRAICHE OR LOW-FAT PLAIN
   YOGURT
1 TSP OF HONEY (OPTIONAL)
1 CUP OF WATER
ICE

1. Put all ingredients into blender and mix until smooth.

NUTRITION:
ENERGY: 359.2 CALORIES
PROTEIN: 8.6 G
CARBS: 8.2 G
FAT: 3.0 G
IRON: 7.2%
HIGH IN POTASSIUM, VITAMIN B6, VITAMIN C,
   CALCIUM, MANGANESE, PHOSPHORUS, AND
   RIBOFLAVIN.

Green Smoothie Joy!

Blueberry Ice Cream Smoothie

1 CUP OF BLUEBERRIES
   (OR ANY CHOSEN BERRY)
   (FROZEN IS BEST)
½ A BANANA
1 CUP OF VANILLA OR
   CHOCOLATE ICE CREAM
1 CUP OF MILK
   (APPROXIMATELY)
1 TSP OF HONEY (OPTIONAL)
A SPRINKLE OR TWO OF
   CINNAMON (OPTIONAL)
ICE CUBES

1. Put all the ingredients in the blender, adding the milk last. Add the milk a little at time so you don't make the smoothie too thin. You can add any milk you like—almond would be a good choice.

2. Blend until smooth.

NUTRITION:
ENERGY: 594.9 CALORIES
PROTEIN: 14.7 G
CARBS: 100.2 G
FAT: 17.3 G
HIGH IN POTASSIUM, VITAMIN A, VITAMIN B12,
   VITAMIN C, VITAMIN D, CALCIUM, MANGANESE,
   PANTOTHENIC ACID, PHOSPHORUS, AND
   RIBOFLAVIN.

Sweet Yogurt & Watermelon Smoothie

1 CUP OF GREEK YOGURT WITH
  NATURAL BACTERIA
1 TBSP OF HONEY
2 CUPS OF WATERMELON
½ CUCUMBER (OPTIONAL)
2 DATES (OPTIONAL)
EXTRA WATER IF NECESSARY

1. Blend all together for a thick smoothie.

NUTRITION:
ENERGY: 335.6 CALORIES
PROTEIN: 23.5 G
CARBS: 64.2 G
FAT: 1.7 G
IRON: 6.7%
HIGH IN POTASSIUM, VITAMIN A, VITAMIN B12,
    VITAMIN C, CALCIUM, PANTOTHENIC ACID,
      PHOSPHORUS, THIAMINE, AND RIBOFLAVIN.

Green Smoothie Joy!

Choccy Ginger Banana Smoothie

2   BANANAS
SOME GRATED GINGER
SEVERAL CHUNKS OF DARK
    CHOCOLATE OR 1 TBSP
    OF DARK COCOA POWDER
    (SUGAR-FREE)
1–2 CUPS OF WATER OR MILK OF
    CHOICE
A COUPLE OF ICE CUBES

1. Mix all together in a blender and enjoy.

NUTRITION:
ENERGY: 664.4 CALORIES
PROTEIN: 21.8 G
CARBS: 106.2 G
FAT: 19.6 G
IRON: 8.3%
HIGH IN POTASSIUM, VITAMIN A, VITAMIN B12,
    VITAMIN C, VITAMIN D, CALCIUM, COPPER,
    MAGNESIUM, MANGANESE, PANTOTHENIC ACID,
    PHOSPHORUS, SELENIUM, AND RIBOFLAVIN.

Cinnamon Apple Smoothie

2 APPLES
1 BANANA
1–2 TBSPS OF GREEK YOGURT
    WITH NATURAL BACTERIA
1 TSP OF CINNAMON
1 TSP OF HONEY
1 CUP APPROX OF ALMOND
    MILK (OR WATER AND A
    HANDFUL OF ALMONDS FOR
    A THICKER SMOOTHIE)
ICE

1. Blend all ingredients together until smooth. Add a few cubes of ice as you go and check consistency.

NUTRITION:
ENERGY: 522 CALORIES
PROTEIN: 22.7 G
CARBS: 105.2 G
FAT: 4.6 G
IRON: 9.4%
HIGH IN POTASSIUM, VITAMIN B6, VITAMIN
    C, VITAMIN D, VITAMIN E, CALCIUM, AND
      PHOSPHORUS.

Green Smoothie Joy!

Index

Green Smoothie Joy!

Metric and Imperial Conversions
(These conversions are rounded for convenience)

Ingredient	Cups/Tablespoons/Teaspoons	Ounces	Grams/Milliliters
Fruit, dried	1 cup	4 ounces	120 grams
Fruits or veggies, chopped	1 cup	5 to 7 ounces	145 to 200 grams
Fruits or veggies, pureed	1 cup	8.5 ounces	245 grams
Honey, maple syrup, or corn syrup	1 tablespoon	.75 ounce	20 grams
Liquids: cream, milk, water, or juice	1 cup	8 fluid ounces	240 ml
Oats	1 cup	5.5 ounces	150 grams
Spices: cinnamon, cloves, ginger, or nutmeg (ground)	1 teaspoon	0.2 ounce	5 ml

Oven Temperatures

Fahrenheit	Celcius	Gas Mark
225°	110°	¼
250°	120°	½
275°	140°	1
300°	150°	2
325°	160°	3
350°	180°	4
375°	190°	5
400°	200°	6
425°	220°	7
450°	230°	8

Rawmazing Desserts
Delicious and Easy Raw Food Recipes for Cookies, Cakes, Ice Cream, and Pie
by Susan Powers

When you eat raw, even your dessert can provide you with essential antioxidants, vitamins, phyto-nutrients, and minerals. With Susan Powers's *Rawmazing Desserts*, you can indulge your sweet tooth, because all of her desserts are whipped up using all-natural ingredients that can improve your health and satisfy cravings. The book includes an abundance of recipes you wouldn't expect to be raw, such as cookies, cakes, cupcakes, custards, mousses, pies, confections, and ice cream. *Rawmazing Desserts* is the perfect cookbook for raw food enthusiasts, or those looking to try something new and healthy. These desserts are sure to charm even the pickiest palate for everyday treats and special occasions alike.

$14.95 Paperback • ISBN 978-1-61608-629-9